CRJ 700

AIRCRAFT SYSTEMS

STUDY GUIDE

A Complete Systems Oral Exam Guide
for the CRJ 700 Pilot

Aviation Study Made Easy

By Aaron Boone

Boone and Rile Publishing [boonerilepublishing.com]

CRJ 700 Aircraft Systems Study Guide
By Aaron Boone
www.crjstudyguide.com

Aaron Boone has logged over 6,500 hours in 13 years of flying as a pilot. He holds an ATP, CFI, CFII
and MEI pilot certificates. Aaron holds four type ratings, CL-65 Canadair Regional Jet, EMB-120
Brasilia, CE-500 and CE-560XL.

Printed in the USA
ISBN 978-0-9790767-3-2

**The purpose of this book is to assist pilots in preparing for a CRJ700 training event. The user
of this information assumes all risk and liability arising from such use. Your company material,
procedures and manuals should be the final authority.**

**While every attempt is made to ensure that the information in this manual is correct, no liability
can be accepted by the author or publisher for loss, damage or injury caused by any errors in, or
omissions from, the information given.**

Please visit us at www.crjstudyguide.com.

Cover Design, Interior Book Design and Production by Studio 6 Sense • info@6sense.net

Contents

Receive your revisions to this book via email.
Please sign up for our newsletter at
www.crjstudyguide.com

Aviation Study Made Easy

his is the most complete CRJ 700 study guide on the market. This guide is laid out in a question/answer format, containing over 1,200 questions and answers on the CRJ 700 systems that will challenge your brain more than multiple-choice or reading a manual.

Preparing for a checkride by skimming through an aircraft manual is ineffective and unfocused. It is very easy to miss important information, fall asleep, or get side tracked. This study guide has taken all of the important information and put it into a simple question and answer format. Unnecessary information has been left out.

The goal of this book is to make your study time more effective so you don't have to spend as much time preparing.

The Aviation Study Made Easy System will allow you to find the specific information you need to work on. After finding these areas, you won't waste a minute going over material you already know. This will help in your recurrent training because you have identified the information that you most easily forget.

You don't need a great memory. What does it take to make good grades in college or smoothly get through the CRJ 700 oral exam? The answer is study habits, study skills, and memory. Sure, some people are smarter than others and have to spend less time studying, but what it comes down to is study habits, study skills, and memory.

Study habits and skills. Let's look at study habits and skills (SHS). If you are learning to fly a CRJ 700, your SHS are probably fairly good. From what I've noticed, though, most pilots still need a little more help. Many pilots spend too much time going over material they already know. When a pilot says, "I'm going to read that chapter again," they are wasting a lot of valuable time going over information they already know. Even if you highlight the important material, you still have to determine if it is information you need to review again, and that takes time, time you may not have to spare.

So how do you quickly eliminate material you already know? Putting all of the information into questions with answers solves this problem. After going through the questions once, you will have marked and eliminated 40-60% of them. The second time through you can focus 100% of your time on the rest of the information. By the time you go through this guide a third time, you can focus 100% of your time on maybe 15% of the information. The amount of information each pilot will eliminate will be different, but the main idea is that no time is spent on information you already know.

If you can eliminate all or most of the questions in this study guide, you will not have a problem with the oral. You can go into the exam with confidence because you have proven to yourself that you can answer all of the questions in this guide. I bet you haven't gone into a checkride with that much confidence before.

Memory. When it comes to memory, some pilots have a better one than others. This means that they have to be exposed to the information less than others to fully retain it. With this study guide, you can focus 100% of your time on the information you don't have in your memory. Sure, it may take you a little more work than the pilot with a better memory, but you are using your time efficiently. In fact, you may be ready for your training event before someone with a better memory if you use this system and they just study by reviewing and re-reading the chapters in their manuals.

This is the system I used in college, and it worked. I was much more organized, and I knew when my studying was done and I was ready for the test. When I then took the test, I usually made an A.

How to best use this book. You need to have 3-4 different colored markers. Go through the book in its entirety. Cover the answer and try to form your own response to the question. If you answer the question correctly, and you don't think you will forget it before your checkride, then mark the question with a particular color. If you did not answer the question correctly, leave it unmarked and go to the next. Do this throughout the entire guide.

When you are done with the first read-through, start over and review only the questions that were not marked. If you answer an unmarked question correctly, and you don't think you will forget it by your checkride, mark the question with a second, different color. Do this over and over. Soon you will only have a few questions that are not marked and these are the ones you are having the most difficulty memorizing or understanding.

You ask, "Why the different color markers?" This will help in later training events because the different colors will identify the questions you had the most difficulty with. You may only need to focus on the questions that took two or three readings.

Depending on your airline training department, some questions may have a very unlikely chance of being asked. If you are sure that your training department will not ask a certain question, mark it with a particular color to identify this. Some training departments want a pilot to know all the details about an aircraft and some do not. I wanted the book to be thorough with all of the systems information so each pilot could decide how to best use the information.

I think you will find the Aviation Study Made Easy System very useful. Training really can be fun, efficient, and less stressful.

Check Ride
Tips

F **ind your pace:** During a checkride, pilots usually perform at different speeds, leading to inconsistency and mistakes. Mistakes most likely occur when the pilot speeds up due to the pressure of the situation. Everyone gets nervous before and during a checkride, it is human nature. Controlling this nervousness will help you perform better.

There is really no malfunction or situation in the simulator that requires you to execute a decision and checklist at the speed of light. You can do what is required of you at the same pace you do any normal procedure. Remember, being accurate is much more beneficial than speed. Also, what you feel as slow in an emergency is actually a perfectly acceptable speed.

Handle a malfunction at the same pace as you do anything else while flying the aircraft. Think of the pace at which you execute a normal checklist, perform a normal takeoff, or perform a descent checklist. These are low-pressure situations and you perform these tasks at a nice smooth pace.

An engine failure at V1 can be handled at this same pace. Take a second to think through the malfunction, then react like you where taught to at the pace you do any other checklist.

When you call for or read a checklist, do it at a normal pace similar to speaking or reading. You will find that your thinking is much clearer and more accurate. You may feel like you are going slowly, but this is a good thing.

Almost any problem that occurs in the aircraft there is a profile, a checklist, or is laid out in a procedure exactly how the pilot is to handle it. Just execute it at a smooth pace and you probably won't have a problem.

Think. When you are executing a normal or emergency checklist, think about what you are doing. When a pilot gets comfortable after many hours in the aircraft, it is a tendency to do and say things out of routine or just try to get the checklist done. For example, when the checklist tells you to turn the left main generator off, think before you grab. Some pilots tend to just reach up to the electrical control panel and grab a switch, sometimes it is the wrong switch. Take a second to think before you execute any part of a checklist. You will find that you are a much more accurate pilot. When you think for a second, you will also find that you slow down your pace.

I hope these tips help make your next checkride less stressful and more successful.

chapter 1

Air Conditioning and Pressurization

What part of the engines supply bleed air to the packs?

Bleed air is supplied from either the engine compressor 6th or 10th stage.

Where are the two air conditioning packs located?

They are located in the aft equipment bay.

What is the maximum operating altitude for single pack?

31,000 feet

What monitors and controls the air conditioning and bleed air systems?

Operation is controlled by two dual channel air conditioning system controllers (ACSC). The left side is controlled by ACSC 1 and the right side by ACSC 2.

Are both channels of the dual channel ACSC required for operation?

Only one is active at any one time. There is no indication as to which channel is active.

Which pack does ACSC 2 control?

ACSC 1 controls the left pack and ACSC 2 controls the right pack.

What does ACSC 1 control?

The left engine bleed system is controlled by ACSC 1 and the right engine bleed system is controlled by ACSC 2. The ACSC control the pack operations, pneumatic valves and temperature control.

Explain the AUTO position of the BLEED VALVES selector.

All aspects of bleed air operation and management is done by the air conditioning system controller (ACSC).

Explain the MANUAL position of the BLEED VALVES selector.

The MANUAL position activates the BLEED SOURCE rotary selector and the ISOL switch.

What does the BLEED SOURCE selector do?

The BLEED SOURCE rotary knob selects the source of bleed air.

Does the low-pressure air cart supply air to the packs for the aircraft cooling?

No, the air is sent to the bleed air manifold and then travels to all the outlets.

Where is the connector for external ground air located?

The external ground air connector is aft of the aft cargo bay door.

How do the pilots know when low pressure external ground air is connected?

There is no indication of the external ground air connector on the ECS page. When the air is connected the air pressure readout on the ECS page will indicate pressure to show the air is connected.

What must be done before the low-pressure air can be turned on?

The main cabin door or avionics bay door must be open.

How are the pack heat exchangers cooled?

The scoop at the base of the vertical stabilizer takes in ram air for cooling. When the aircraft is on the ground a fan pulls air into the scoop. There are two exhaust vents on the rear of the fuselage where the air is discharged.

Where are the temperature sensors located in the cabin?

One monitor is in the front and one in the rear.

What happens when there is a 10°C difference or greater between a temperature sensor and the selected temperature?

The pack is automatically set to high airflow to meet the heating or cooling selection.

After a pack high temperature shutdown can the pack automatically restart?

When the temperature cools the pack will automatically restart.

What does the RECIRC FAN switch do?

This switch controls the recirculation fan in each exhaust duct.

Are both cargo bays pressurized?

Yes, but the aft cargo bay is the only one ventilated with re-circulated cabin air.

What happens when the cargo COND AIR is selected?

An electric heater in the supply duct is activated to keep the aft cargo compartment better suited for animals. The ACSC regulates conditioned air temperature to the aft cargo bay.

How many smoke detectors are located in the front and aft cargo compartments?

The aft cargo bay has two smoke detectors and the forward cargo bay has three.

Is overheat protection provided in the forward cargo compartment?

No, overheat protection is just in the aft.

Explain the OFF position of the cargo switch.

In the off position ventilation to the aft cargo bay is turned off by closing the intake and exhaust valves.

Explain the AIR position of the cargo switch.

Ventilation to the aft cargo bay is provided by opening the intake and exhaust valves. The aft cargo area is ventilated by the ECS system controlled by ACSC 2.

What does an amber CARGO OVHT on the EICAS indicate?

This EICAS message will only occur if the conditioned air option is installed. If the aft cargo bay temperature reaches more than 40° C and conditioned air is selected, an overheat condition is detected. The heater is de-energized and the AFT CARGO OVHT is displayed. The CARGO COND AIR switch should be selected to FAN.

When there is an AFT CARGO OVHT with the condition air option, and the cargo fan switch is selected from COND AIR to FAN, what does this do?

This takes the power away from the over temperature circuitry and removes the indication from the EICAS display. This cargo intake and exhaust SOVs are still open so there is suitable airflow. It matches the condition since the heater is automatically turned off.

Explain an AFT CARGO SOV status message?

The SOV for inlet air has failed closed or open.

How is the outflow pressurization valve controlled?

The outflow valve is electrically operated by three DC motors that drive a gearbox and actuator to move the valve.

How many outflow valves are installed?

One

How is the outflow valve motors controlled?

The two cabin pressure controllers control two of the motors. There is a third motor that is controlled by the manual mode of the pressurization control panel.

How is the single outflow valve opened and closed?

The outflow valve is moved by one of three DC motors. The two CPCs control two of the motors (each controlling one motor) and the third motor is controlled by the manual pressurization control.

Which air data computer (ADC) provides inputs to the pressure controllers?

Normally ADC 1 is the primary with ADC 2 as the backup.

How is over pressure and negative pressure protection provided?

On the aft bulkhead there are two pneumatic safety valves that provide this protection. These valves operate independently of the AUTO and MANUAL pressurization modes. The valves are spring loaded to the closed position.

What is the maximum cabin altitude rate of change?

The cabin altitude rate of change is limited to a maximum of 300-750 fpm when descending and 500-800 fpm when climbing.

When the AUTO mode of the cabin pressurization is selected, what controls the pressurization?

One of two CPCs control all phases of pressurization at a given time. The CPC that is not active will be in standby and will become active if there is a failure of the active CPC.

What indicates which CPC is active?

The active CPC is identified on the ECS page.

When will the active CPC become the standby CPC?

The active CPC can be changed at any time manually by pressing the PRESS CONTROL switchlight on the CABIN PRESS control panel two times. Automatically the active will become the standby three minutes after landing. The CPCs change upon each landing automatically.

What are the automatic modes of the CPCs?

- Ground mode
- Takeoff mode
- Flight abort mode
- Climb/Cruise mode
- Descent mode
- Landing mode
- Touch and go mode

Explain the ground mode of the CPC.

After AC power is applied the CPC completes a self-test. The ground mode will start at the completion of the self-test and the ground valve and outflow valve will be driven full open to ensure the cabin is not pressurized.

Explain the takeoff mode of the CPC.

The takeoff mode is activated when the thrust levers are set for takeoff. The outflow valve start to close and the cabin will be pressurized. The pre-pressurization of the aircraft eliminates any noticeable pressure bumps. If the takeoff is done without pressurization the outflow valve and ground valve will be closed.

What will the CPC do if a takeoff is aborted?

If the thrust levers are retarded during an aborted takeoff, the cabin will depressurize at 500 fpm for 20 seconds. After the 20 seconds the outflow valve will be full open. The CPC will then be in ground mode.

Explain the flight abort mode of the CPC.

This mode is armed within the first 10 minutes of the flight and the aircraft is still below 6000 feet. The purpose of this mode is so the pilot does not have to reset the landing elevation when returning to the departure field. The mode is activated with a decent of 1000 fpm or more.

Explain the climb/cruise mode of the CPC.

The CPC controls cabin pressurization based on the selected landing field elevation and a theoretical schedule of cabin altitude versus aircraft altitude. The profile that the cabin climbs on is based on the aircraft's rate of climb, which that profile is about 500-800 fpm. During cruise there is an assigned cabin altitude for every cruising altitude. Once in cruise mode the descent mode is armed automatically.

Explain the descent mode of the CPC.

The cabin will descend based on the rate of descent and flight time remaining. Flight time remaining is based on information received from the ADCs. The cabin will normally descend at 300-750 fpm until the cabin altitude is at the selected landing field elevation or the maximum differential, whichever is higher.

What is different about the descent mode of the CPC if the landing elevation is above 8,000 feet?

The CPC will maintain the cabin at maximum differential until the descent begins. At that time the cabin altitude will increase to the landing elevation set.

Explain the landing mode of the CPC.

When the PSEU senses weight on wheels and the thrust levers are at idle the CPC will transfer from the descent mode to landing mode. In the landing mode the CPC will climb the cabin at 600 fpm for 30 seconds and then enter the ground mode. Three minutes after landing the active CPC will become the standby.

Explain the touch and go mode of the CPC.

If the thrust levers are advanced after touchdown, the system will enter the pre-pressure mode.

What does the FAULT light in the PRESS CONT switchlight indicate?

Both CPCs have failed.

Explain what happens when the EMER DEPRESS switchlight is pressed on the CABIN PRESS control panel.

The active CPC will drive the outflow valve fully open. If the aircraft is below 14,250 feet the aircraft will completely depressurize and if it is above 14,250 feet the aircraft cabin will climb and maintain 14,250 +/- 750 feet. Both CPCs have emergency depressurization circuitry that is not part of the normal system so it will not be affected by normal system failures.

What valve ensures the aircraft is depressurized on the ground?

The ground valve ensures the aircraft is depressurized on the ground. The ground valve also aids in exhausting avionics cooling air.

When does the ground valve open and close?

The valve closes when the service and passenger doors are closed. The valve will open after touchdown plus 60 seconds. The valve is closed during flight.

How is the avionics equipment in the avionics bay cooled?

The exhaust air from the cockpit and cabin is circulated to cool the avionics equipment in the avionics bay.

How is the air used for avionics cooling moved around and exhausted?

Exhaust fans accomplish movement of the cooling air. The air is exhausted through the ground valve while on the ground and through the outflow valve while in flight.

What does the STBY position on the display-cooling panel do?

This will remove power from the two display fans. Cooling airflow will now be provided by conditioned air from the cockpit duct.

Can animals be carried in the forward cargo?

No

What are the sources of air conditioning bleed air?

- APU
- Engines
- External air cart

What engine stage normally provides bleed air?

6th

What determines if the 6th or 10th stage is used for bleed air?

The air conditioning system controller (ACSC) determines which stage is used for bleed air.

When is the 6th and 10th stage used at the same time?

Never

What does it take to open and close the 6th stage engine bleed valve?

The 6th stage engine bleed valve needs bleed air and electricity to open.

When insufficient pressure is supplied by the 6th stage, what will happen?

The high pressure valve (HPV) will open to supply higher pressure bleed air from the 10th stage.

What will happen if a high demand of bleed air is needed, more than the 6th stage can provide?

The HPV will open and higher pressure from the 10th stage is provided.

When will the high pressure valve (HPV) close?

- ACSC signal is lost.
- Engines are shutdown.
- The associated ENG FIRE PUSH is selected.
- Bleed leak.
- Over pressure.
- When the manual override lever is used.

Does the EICAS indicate the position of the high pressure valves (HPV)?

There is no indication of the HPV.

What normally determines the position of the APU LCV?

ACSC1 normally controls the APU LCV but if it fails the APU LCV will be controlled by ACSC2.

What controls the position of the APU LCV?

The APU electronic control unit (ECU) is what controls the position of the LCV. The ACSC gives the signals to the ECU to open or close.

What position will the APU LCV fail to?

Closed

What type of control logic is provided for the APU LCV by the ACSC?

- The ACSC will ensure that the engine bleed valves are closed before the APU LCV is opened.
- The ACSC will not allow the APU to supply bleed air to the anti-ice system.

During MANUAL mode operation, when will the APU LCV open?

- The BLEED SOURCE switch is selected to APU.
- APU is running and able to accept bleed air loading.
- BLEED VALVES switch is in MANUAL.

What is the changeover point for the bleeds after takeoff?

The point where the bleeds change from the APU if operating to the engines is when the gear is up, flaps at 20 degrees or less and the thrust levers are set to the CLIMB position. The transfer will take about 20 seconds and is automatic.

When is bleed air switched back to the APU on approach?

If the APU operating and available for bleed air loading the transfer occurs when the gear is down or flaps greater than 20 degrees. The transfer takes about 20 seconds and is automatic.

In AUTO mode what happens if the APU is supplying bleed air and the wing and/or cowl anti-ice are selected on?

This will close the APU LCV and the engines will supply bleed air.

In MANUAL mode what happens if the APU is supplying bleed air and the wing and/or cowl anti-ice are selected on?

The automatic transfer of bleed air from the APU to the engines is not available. If the wing and/or cowl anti-icing is selected to ON the following will occur:

- The APU LCV will stay open.
- BLEED MISCONFIG caution message.
- The engine bleed valves stay closed.
- Cowl anti-ice valves will open.
- Wing anti-ice valves will not open and remain closed.

Does the APU feed both packs bleed air?

The APU supplies bleed air to the left pack. The ISOL valve can be opened to allow the APU to feed bleed air to both packs.

The left engine normally supplies bleed air to which pack?

The packs normally receive bleed air from the onside engine. The left engine normally supplies the left pack.

What controls the pressure regulating shutoff valves (PRSOVs)?

ACSC 1 controls the left engine PRSOV and ACSC 2 controls the right engine PRSOV. The PRSOVs are opened by the pack switchlights on the AIR CONDITIONING panel.

What allows a single bleed air source to feed both packs?

The isolation valve (ISOL). This valve is controlled by the ISOL switch on the BLEED AIR panel. The BLEED VALVES selector must be in MANUAL for the ISOL switch to be enabled.

What are the basic components of a pack?

There are four basic components of an air conditioning pack. They are the air cycle machine (ACM), dual heat exchangers, re-heater and a condenser.

How is the pack heat exchangers cooled?

The scoop at the base of the vertical stabilizer takes in ram air for cooling. When the aircraft is on the ground a fan pulls air into the scoop. There are two exhaust vents on the rear of the fuselage where the air is discharged.

What is the purpose of the ram air scoop at the base of the vertical stabilizer?

Air enters this scoop and is used as the cooling means for the air-to-air heat exchangers. The ram air flows across the pre-cooler and dual heat exchangers thus cooling the pack air. The cooling ram air exits through the vents located on the lower right and left sides of the fuselage in the aft area. When the aircraft is on the ground there is no ram air to enter the scoop, so a fan that is driven by the air cycle machine draws the air in the scoop.

The hydraulic system heat exchanger for system 1 and 2 also receives cooling air through this duct.

Explain the RAM AIR switchlight on the air conditioning panel.

This switchlight controls the ram air shut off valve. When selected open, it will direct air that enters the ram air scoop to enter the left distribution duct. This duct will ventilate the flight deck and cool the EFIS and EICAS equipment. Only a small portion will ventilate the cabin. This switch will only work with the packs off.

What cools the hot air for the air conditioning system?

An air cycle machine and heat exchangers cools the hot compressed air.

Where is the cabin air exhausted?

The air sent under the floor to the outflow valve on the aft pressure bulkhead.

At what pack temperature does the amber EICAS message L PACK HI TEMP appear?

When the pack temperature reaches 85°C the L PACK HI TEMP will appear.

When would ram air ventilation be used?

When both packs have failed in flight ram air ventilation would be used.

What is a caution when operating in MANUAL temperature control?

There is no temperature protection so a PACK HI TEMP condition and icing the pack water separator is possible. At 85°C the PACK HI TEMP caution message will appear and the pack will shut down. If the temperature is below 3°C the water separator can ice up and cause it to cycle pack output.

How are the EFIS and EICAS cathode ray tubes (CRTs) cooled?

The CRTs are cooled by air-conditioned pack air distributed by fans.

Explain the DISPLAY FAN selector on the avionics cooling control panel.

The CRTs for the EFIS and EICAS require three AC powered fans to ensure there is proper airflow for display cooling. If a CRT overheats it has internal overheat protection which will shut down the affected CRT. The three fans are controlled by the PSEU and weight-on-wheels.

One fan is used in flight and the other fan is used on the ground. The switching is accomplished by the PSEU and the weight on wheel function. If fan 1 fails in flight, fan 2 can be selected by the FLT ALTN position of the DSPLY FAN knob. If both fans fail, the STBY fan can be selected. This will activate the standby fan that draws air from the flight deck air conditioning duct. The GND ALTN position will activate the other fan if the main ground fan fails.

Failure is indicated by an amber DISPLAY COOL on the EICAS.

Explain the operation of the AVIONICS FAN switch.

Cooling air is needed for avionics bay cooling. Two fans are used for this, one for flight and one on the ground. Switching is a function of the PSEU WOW signal sent for takeoff and landing. The air used for cooling is taken from under the cabin floor and is the recalculated passenger cabin air.

If fan 1 for flight fails, fan 2 can be selected by moving the AVIONICS FAN switch to FLT ALTN. If the aircraft is on the ground and fan 2 fails, fan 1 can be select by selecting GRD ALTN. Failure or low airflow is indicated by an amber AVIONICS FAN on the EICAS.

Explain the NORM position of the AVIONICS FAN selector.

The appropriate fan will automatically be selected for flight or ground operations avionics cooling. Fan 1 is for flight and 2 is for ground operations.

What does an AVIONICS FAN caution message indicate?

Low airflow in the exhaust ducts or the avionics fan has failed.

Explain the FLT ALTN position of the AVIONICS FAN selector.

The ground fan will operate in flight instead of the flight fan.

Explain the GRD ALTN position of the AVIONICS FAN selector.

The flight fan will operate on the ground instead of the ground fan.

Explain the NORM position of the DSPLY FAN selector.

The appropriate fan will automatically be selected for flight or ground operations to cool the CRT displays. Fan 1 is for flight and 2 is for ground operations.

Explain the FLT ALTN position of the DSPLY FAN selector.

The ground fan will operate in flight instead of the flight fan.

Explain the GRD ALTN position of the DSPLY FAN selector.

The flight fan will operate on the ground instead of the ground fan.

Explain the STBY position of the DSPLY FAN selector.

This position is used when both display fans fail. When the STBY position is selected cooling air is taken from the flight deck air conditioning duct.

Explain the avionics exhaust fan.

There is a single fan that operates when the AC buses are powered. It extracts the exhaust air from the CRTs, the avionics racks, the pedestal panel and the avionics bay.

When the passenger door or the service door is open the exhaust air is discharged through the overboard exhaust valve. If this valve fails open when the passenger and service doors are closed, an amber OVBD COOL will be displayed on the EICAS. Under this condition the aircraft will not pressurize properly.

With the passenger and service doors closed, the overboard exhaust valve closes. The inboard exhaust valve opens to send the air into the fuselage around the under floor area in the aft of the aircraft.. An EICAS status message INBD COOL FAIL will indicate failure of this valve.

Will there be any warning if there is a low airflow condition for CRT cooling?

An EICAS caution message DISPLAY COOL will appear if there is low airflow in the exhaust ducts or CRT 1 or 2 fan failure.

What does an OVBD COOL FAIL status message indicate?

The passenger and service doors are not locked and the overboard exhaust valve is closed.

What would be an indication of a PFD/MFD over temperature condition?

A red DISPLAY TEMP warning will appear on the PFD or MFD to indicate a thermal shutdown is approaching. If it is the PFD the ground and sky raster is removed from the PFD to delay the shutdown.

What provides ventilation to the lavatory and galley?

Any time AC power is available exhaust fans will provide ventilation to the lavatory and galley.

What does an inoperative exhaust fan in the lavatory or galley indicate?

AC power must be available for the fan to operate. The fans have an overheat switch that will shut down the fan if the fan motor overheats.

Explain the HEATER switchlight in the galley.

The galley has a 1,000 WATT heater in the galley air supply line to help heat the galley and the area around the service door.

What would happen if the galley heater output became too hot?

The power to the heater will be removed. This overheat switch is self-resetting.

What would happen if the internal temperature of the galley heater reached an overheat condition?

The heater would be disabled by an overheat protection switch.

What is the maximum pressure differential?

8.7 psi

Explain the manual mode of the cabin pressurization.

The electric motor assigned to the manual control of the outflow valve is used to open and close the valve. The MAN ALT knob is used on the CABIN PRESS control panel.

Explain how you would manually control the pressurization.

Pressing the PRESS CONT switchlight once on the CABIN PRESS control panel will illuminate the MAN light in the switchlight and activate manual pressurization control. Using the MAN RATE knob and the MAN ALT selector valve, the pilot can manually control the outflow valve and therefore control cabin pressurization. Selecting up or down on the MAN ALT selector will climb or descend the cabin at the rate selected on the MAN RATE knob. The EICAS primary, ECS and status page will provide pressurization information. Begin manual pressurization control with rate knob at full decrease to avoid large pressure changes at manual activation.

What does the red FAULT in the PRESS CONT switchlight indicate?

The light indicates that both CPCs have failed.

What does an APU BLEED ON caution message indicate?

The APU bleed is on above 27,000 feet.

What does a L or R ENG BLEED caution message indicate?

The high pressure valve, pressure regulating SOV or controller has failed.

What happens when the pressurization control switch is pressed once?

Manual mode is selected.

What happens when the manual cabin altitude regulator is selected up with the manual pressurization selected?

The outflow valve will open and the cabin altitude will climb.

When manual pressurization is selected where will the pressurization readouts be displayed?

The primary page of the EICAS and the ECS page will display pressurization information.

What does the amber FAULT light in the left or right pack switchlight indicate?

A fault has occurred in the respective pack. The fault could be an over temperature or over pressure condition.

What does a L or R PACK TEMP caution message indicate?

An under-temperature less than 3°C or an over-temperature greater than 85°C while in manual mode.

What does a white 24 in the temperature position on the ECS page indicate?

No data is available.

What differential pressure range is maintained during aircraft operations?

The outflow valves will open and close to maintain a differential pressure from 0 to 8.6 PSID.

Explain the protection against excessive differential pressure.

If the pressure differential reaches 8.6 +/- 1, an aural warning "cabin pressure" will sound and the outflow valve will automatically open to bring the differential pressure back to the normal range. If there is a negative pressure differential that reaches -0.5 PSID, the outflow valve will automatically open to bring the pressure into the normal range. There is no EICAS indication for exceeding the negative pressure differential of -0.5.

What is the purpose of the cabin pressure acquisition module (CPAM)?

The CPAM provides pressurization data for display on the EICAS after communicating with the data concentrator units (DCU). The EICAS indications include differential pressure (D), cabin altitude (CALT) and cabin rate of climb or descent (RATE).

When the cabin altitude exceeds 8,500 feet the CPAM will display an amber CABIN ALT on the EICAS. When the cabin altitude exceeds 10,000 feet the CPAM will display a red CABIN ALT on the EICAS and an aural "cabin pressure" alert.

When cabin altitude exceeds 10,000 feet the CPAM will illuminate the NO SMOKING/ FASTEN SEAT BELT sign if those switches are in AUTO.

When the cabin altitude reaches 14,000 feet the CPAM will send the signal to drop the passenger oxygen masks.

Will any of the normal CPAM functions occur if the CPAM fails?

The CPC that is in standby will generate all the EICAS messages if the CPAM fails, but the illumination of the SEATBELT/ NO SMOKING signs and dropping of the passenger masks will not occur.

Note: This would automatically occur if the CPAM were operating when the cabin altitude exceeds 10,000 and 14,000 feet respectively. For the SEATBELT/ NO SMOKING signs to illuminate automatically, the switches would need to be in AUTO.

When will the cabin altitude aural warning be heard?

When cabin altitude is above 10,000 feet.

What happens if the CPAM fails?

The standby CPC takes over but the CPC can't drop the masks or illuminate the NO SMOKING/SEATBELT SIGNS. The CPAM normally illuminates the SMOKING/SEATBELT SIGNS if the cabin altitude exceeds 10,000 feet and sends the signal to drop the passenger masks at 14,000 feet.

Where are the pressurization readouts during manual mode operation?

During manual pressurization operation C ALT, RATE and ΔP will be displayed on the primary page of the EICAS. When the pressurization is in automatic mode the pressurization readouts will be displayed on the EICAS status page.

What does a CABIN ALT WARN HI status message indicate?

The landing field elevation is set above 8.000 feet.

What does an OUTFLOW VLV OPEN status message indicate?

The outflow valve is fully open.

When will the cabin altitude readout turn amber?

When the cabin altitude is above 8,500 feet the cabin altitude readout will turn amber.

When will the cabin altitude readout turn red?

When the cabin altitude is above 10,000 feet the cabin altitude readout will turn red.

On the ECS page what is the difference in white and green pressurization data?

The monitored data is in green and active data is in white.

What regulates the pressure of the air from the 10th stage before it enters the pack?

Due to the extreme pressure of the air from the 6th and 10th stage, the air could damage the pack if the pressure was not reduced. This is the job of the pack pressure regulating shutoff valve (PRSOV) and is used to reduce the pressure of the air before it enters the pack.

How does the PRSOV help a single pack supply sufficient pressure to the flight deck and the cabin during single pack operations?

There are two pressure settings, one for dual pack and one for single pack. When two packs are available, the PRSOVs reduce the pressure to a normal pressure. During single pack operations the single PRSOV will increase the operating pressure, which will permit the single pack to supply the cabin and flight deck with sufficient airflow. It will not be at the same volume as with both packs operating.

Where is the air distributed that comes from the left and right pack?

The left pack will normally supply the cockpit and the right pack will supply the cabin.

During single pack operations what allows the pack to provide air to the cabin and cockpit?

A mixing manifold allows the single pack to provide air to the cabin and cockpit.

What supplies the cooling air for the heat exchangers?

The ram air scoop at the base of the vertical stabilizer is where cooling air enters. The air is then exhausted overboard through two vents on the rear of the fuselage. When the aircraft is on the ground, a fan pulls air into the ram air scoop.

What is the altitude limit for extracting bleed air from the APU for air conditioning? What will happen if the APU is used for bleed air above this altitude?

The limit is 27,000 feet. If this altitude is exceeded the EICAS caution message APU BLEED AIR ON will appear.

Is overheat protection provided in the cargo bay?

Overheat protection is provided only with the condition air option selected.

Where is the cabin pressurization monitoring source indicated?

The monitoring source is identified on the ECS page just below and to the left of the APU symbol. The monitoring source is normally the CPAM.

What becomes the monitoring source if the CPAM fails?

The standby pressure controller is the monitoring source if the CPAM fails. If all monitoring sources fail amber dashes will replace the monitoring source identification on the ECS page.

chapter 2

Automatic Flight Controls

Explain the optimized pitch of the flight director (FD) for takeoff.

The pitch of the fight director (FD) is based on the flap setting and the ratio of VR to V2. This produces a pitch angle that is unique for that set of conditions.

What speed is the takeoff pitch of the FD optimized for?

The pitch is between 11-18 degrees and is optimized to obtain V2 + 10.

What would you do if the FD were deferred?

Refer to the Supplemental Procedures to determine pitch attitudes. Refer to the MEL and follow your company procedures.

What occurs to the FD if an engine fails on takeoff?

The FD pitch will change to about 10 to 14 degrees for optimum pitch attitude to maintain V2.

What conditions will cause the FD bars to not appear when the TOGA button is pressed for takeoff?

- If the pilot enters VR and V2 and the difference is greater than 24 knots between both settings.
- If the flaps were not set to 8 or 20 degrees for takeoff.

All of these conditions will display a red FD flag on the PFDs.

Is the go-around pitch of the FD optimized?

No, the pitch is set to 8 degrees.

What two systems are integrated by the automatic flight control system (AFCS)?

Flight director and the autopilot systems.

What four systems does the AFCS supply information to?

- Dual flight directors

- Two axis autopilot

- Automatic pitch trim

- Two yaw dampers

What are the four system components of the AFCS?

- Flight control panel (FCP)

- Two flight control computers (FCC)

- Two autopilot servomotors

- Two yaw dampers

What are the main AFCS microprocessors and where are they located?

Flight control computers (FCC) 1 and 2. They are located in the IAPS.

What systems do the FCCs provide instructions to?

- FCP

- FDs

- Yaw dampers

- AP servo motors

The flight director receives its position on the primary flight display (PFD) from what systems?

FCCs

What is the IAPS?

The integrated avionics processing system. This system contains many computers and components and provides the means for them to communicate.

Are both FDs always active?

During most modes, one flight director is supplying guidance information to both PFDs. The other FD is in standby but they do continue to continuously cross talk. During the following modes, both FDs are active and providing onside information:

- Takeoff mode
- Approach mode
- Go around mode

What occurs if the active FD fails?

A white FD1 or FD 2 FAIL EICAS status message will be displayed. Also a red FD in a box will appear on the PFDs.

Where is the vertical and lateral mode selections of the FD displayed?

On the flight mode annunciator (FMA), located at the top of the PFDs.

Explain the two fields of the FMA?

A vertical cyan line separates the two fields, with the left side the active field and the right side the armed field. The top line of the FMA displays the active and armed FD lateral mode and the bottom line the active and armed FD vertical mode. The active side is green text and the armed side is white text.

What information do the FCCs process to figure the flight of the aircraft?

The information needed comes from the attitude and heading reference system (AHRS) and the air data computer (ADC).

What happens if information in the FMA field is invalid?

If any information is invalid, it is indicated by a red line where the text would be.

When can only one FD command bar be removed from the PFDs and when will both FD command bars be removed by a selection of the FD button on the FCP?

Selection of the FD FCP button on the side that is not active will remove the FD command bars from that side only. Selection of the FD FCP button on the side that is active will remove both FD command bars.

If the autopilot (AP) is engaged, will deselecting the FD button on the active side disengage the AP?

No, the onside FD button is inactive and deselecting it will not disengage the AP. If the off-side FD button is pressed, the FD bars on the off-side will be removed and will not disengage the AP.

What is the purpose of the XFR button on the FCP?

This button selects the active FD in some modes. It can also be stated that it selects which FCC will command the FDs in some modes. Remember that some modes, the onside FCC will command only the onside FD. (Example: APPR mode)

What FD modes are both FDs active and display information received from the onside FCC?

- Takeoff mode (TOTO)
- Approach mode (APPR)
- Go around mode (GAGA)

FCC 1 controls FD 1 only and FCC 2 controls FD 2.

What do the FCC status indicator lights on the flight control panel (FCP) indicate?

When a mode button is selected the request is sent to the FCCs and if the FCCs determine that all conditions are met for that function, the green lights will illuminate. The light to the left of the respective button indicates FCC 1 has acknowledged the request and the light to the right that FCC 2 has acknowledged the request.

What does the flight director synchronization switch (FD SYNC) do when the AP is engaged?

Nothing

What is the purpose of the FD SYNC switch?

When the AP is not engaged, it synchronizes vertical and lateral values at the time of selection.

What happens when the FD SYNC button is pressed and released while the FD has an active vertical mode?

There is a yellow SYNC message in the armed field of the FMA and it will stay there for 3 seconds. The FD is synchronized to the current aircraft vertical mode selected and the FD will maintain this pitch even if the actual aircraft pitch is changed. Ex: If IAS is selected and the FD SYNC is pressed, the FD will match the current pitch to maintain the current IAS.

What happens when the FD SYNC button is pressed and held while the FD has an active vertical mode?

There is a yellow SYNC message in the armed field of the FMA and it will stay there until the SYNC button is released. The FD is synchronized to the current aircraft pitch and bank and it will maintain synchronized even if the aircraft changes its pitch and bank.

How do you disable the active lateral mode of the FD?

Re-select the active FCP button or select another lateral mode.

What heading will the FD maintained when the TOGA switch is pressed on a go-around?

The FD will hold the heading at the time of activation.

Explain the take-off mode of the FMA when the aircraft is on the ground?

Pressing the TOGA button will display a green TO in the vertical and lateral active mode of the FMA. This is achieved by pressing one of the TOGA switches prior to the take-off roll. The lateral mode will hold the heading at weight off wheels. The vertical mode will be optimized for the specific conditions of each takeoff. The pitch will be between 11 to 18 degrees.

Pressing the TOGA button will also update the position in the FMS.

What is the default lateral mode of the FD?

Roll mode is the default lateral mode of the FD.

If no lateral mode is selected at the time the AP is engaged, what lateral mode will the AP maintain?

If the bank angle is less than 5 degrees, the FD will roll level. If the bank angle is greater than 5 degrees, the FD maintains the bank angle at the time of AP engagement.

How can the AP disconnect warning be canceled after the TOGA switch is pressed on a go-around?

Push the TOGA switch again or push the AP disconnect switch on the control wheel.

What occurs to the FD lateral mode if the navigation source is lost?

The FD lateral mode reverts to roll mode.

How are lateral FD modes selected?

The lateral FD modes are activated or armed by buttons on the FCP or the TOGA switches on the thrust levers.

When the localizer captures, what FCP modes will automatically clear if engaged?

It clears the heading mode, half bank, and the turbulence mode.

What course must be set when using the back course mode?

The front course must be set.

How is the go-around mode indicated on the FMA?

The lateral and vertical mode on the active FMA has the green text GA.

Explain the half bank option of the FD?

This mode will restrict the FD bank to 15 degrees. It is automatically selected climbing through 31,600 feet and automatically turned off descending through 31,600 feet. Half bank can be manually selected by the ½ BANK button on the FCP.

It is not available during a go-around mode, takeoff mode, on-side localizer or approach capture.

How is an active vertical mode disabled?

Select another vertical mode, or re-select the active FCP button.

What are the ways to arm or activate a vertical mode?

- The vertical mode buttons like VS on the FCP or the pitch wheel on the FCP. If just the pitch wheel is rotated after a new altitude is selected, pitch mode will be activated.
- TOGA switches.

How is a pre-selected altitude armed when set in the altitude alerter?

When a vertical mode is selected like VS or IAS.

How is the FD altitude capture point determined?

The capture point is determined by the closure rate. With high vertical speeds the capture point is farther from the altitude. If the vertical speed of the aircraft is only 500 fpm then altitude capture occurs within about 50 feet of the selected altitude. If the vertical speed is 3,000 fpm then altitude capture can occur before the 1,000 feet to level off aural tone.

What indicates the half bank mode is engaged?

The lights associated with the 1/2 bank switch are illuminated when engaged. Also there will be a 1/2 BNK message on the PFDs.

Explain the altitude capture process in the FMA?

With a new altitude selected there is a white ALTS in the vertical armed portion of the FMA. When the ALTS mode is captured, the white ALTS disappears and a green ALTS CAP appears in the active vertical portion of the FMA and will flash for 5 seconds and then become steady.

The altitude capture will continue until the aircraft is within 100 feet of the pre-selected altitude. At this point, the ALTS CAP message is replaced with a green flashing ALTS that will also flash for 5 seconds and then becomes steady. The FD is now holding the selected altitude.

How is the altitude alerting system (ALS) connected to the FD and AP systems?

The ALS is independent of the FD and AP system. It processes information from the air data computers (ADC).

During a climb or descent, when will the ALS alert of the impending level off?

The ALS will alert 1,000 feet prior to the pre-selected altitude.

How does the ALS alert of an impending level off?

An aural tone and a flashing ALTS on the FMA indicates an impending level off.

If the FD is tracking an altitude, what warnings will be given if there is an altitude deviation?

If the aircraft deviates by more than 100 feet from the selected altitude, the altitude bugs flash and there will be a series of tones. If the deviation continues, at 1,000 feet from the selected altitude, there will be an aural tone and the altitude bugs and digital readout flash amber.

What are the ten vertical FD modes?

- Pre-select altitude (ALTS)
- Pitch (PTCH)
- Takeoff (TO)
- Go-around (GA)
- Vertical approach mode (GS)
- Vertical speed (VS)
- Speed (IAS)
- Descent (DES)
- Climb (CLB)
- Altitude hold (ALT)

How is the FD pitch mode activated?

If no vertical mode is selected and the AP is engaged, the FD will default to pitch mode. Pitch mode can be engaged by a third press of the SPEED button or by rotating the pitch trim wheel on the FCP with a vertical mode other than VS selected. If an altitude is captured, a new altitude must be selected t activate a vertical mode.

If the aircraft is climbing or descending and the ALT button on the FCP is pressed, what altitude will the FD maintain?

The FD will level and then climb or descend to capture the pressure altitude at the time the ALT mode button was pressed.

What must be done before SPEED mode can be engaged?

A new altitude must be selected in the altitude selector.

How will a speed mode be displayed on the FMA?

Speed mode will be displayed by CLB, DES, IAS or MACH on the FMA. When a speed mode is active an ALTS will be in the vertical armed field of the FMA.

When selecting SPEED mode, how do you select whether the aircraft will climb or descend?

A new pre-selected altitude must be set. Climb or descend depends if the selected altitude is above or below actual altitude.

Explain the difference between a green CLB 250 and an IAS 250 in the active FMA on the PFD.

CLB ### is activated by pressing the SPEED button on the FCP once with a pre-selected altitude set that is above the current altitude. If the target airspeed is increased the FCC will direct the FD to pitch down but never lower than 50 feet per minute (fpm) and then climb once the airspeed is achieved.

IAS ### is activated by a second press of the SPEED button, and the aircraft will maintain the selected airspeed even if it means going from a climb to a descent.

Note: Vertical DES and vertical IAS mode is the same.

What would occur if the SPEED button were pressed consecutively?

The vertical modes will cycle between CLB or DES, IAS and PTCH.

How is IAS ### on the active FMA activated?

By pressing the SPEED button on the FCP twice.

Explain the vertical IAS mode?

A second press of the SPEED button on the FCP activates this mode. A new pre-selected altitude must be selected for the aircraft to leave the altitude hold. If a climb or descent is desired, the thrust levers are increased or decreased and the speed will be maintained. The aircraft will go in the opposite direction of the desired altitude to achieve the target speed. Example: If the selected IAS is higher than the current speed, the FD could command a descent to achieve the target airspeed.

At what altitude is there an automatic change over from indicated airspeed to Mach in the FMA?

The change over occurs at 31,600 feet.

How do you manually change from IAS to Mach on the FMA?

By pressing the center of the SPEED selection knob.

Each click of the pitch trim wheel on the FCP is equal to how many feet?

100 feet

When the TOGA switch is pressed during a go-around, how many degrees pitch-up will the FD command bars indicate?

8 degrees

The TOGA switch is pressed on a go-around, how can the autopilot warning be cancelled?

By pushing the AP disconnect switch on the control wheel or a second press of the TOGA switch.

What control surfaces do the AP servos provide command inputs to?

Only the elevators and ailerons. The rudder is controlled by the yaw damper system.

What conditions must exist for the autopilot to be engaged with the selection of the AP ENG button on the FCP?

- No significant instability of the aircraft exists.
- Both FCCs are working.
- At least one yaw damper is engaged.
- Minimum of one channel of the horizontal stabilizer is engaged and the FCCs determine that there are no faults with the horizontal stabilizer pitch system.

When the AP is engaged, what is the indication of a control surface being significantly out-of- trim?

There is an amber EICAS message indicating whether it is the aileron or the elevator and in what direction. There will also be an amber-boxed E or A on the PFDs.

Caution message: AP Trim is LWD or RWD and AP Trim is ND or NU.

Where is the activation of the TURB mode indicated on the PFD?

There is nothing on the PFD to indicate that the TURB mode is engaged. The only indication is the two green lights on the sides of the TURB button. The lights indicate that the left and right FCCs respectively approve the selection of this mode.

What automatically clears the TURB mode?

A localizer capture clears the TURB mode.

What are the aural and visual indications that the autopilot has been disengaged?

There is a red flashing AP—➤ on the PFD and the autopilot aural warning sounds for approximately 5 seconds.

How can the autopilot be manually disengaged and what warning will be given?

- Pressing the YD DISC pushbutton will disconnect both YDs.
- Pressing either TOGA switch.
- Pressing the AP ENG pushbutton.
- The AP DISC on the FCP.
- The stab trim split switches on the control wheel.
- Either AP/SP DISC button on the control wheels.

There will be the aural warning sound for approximately 5 seconds and the red flashing AP—➤ on the PFD.

If the autopilot system has a fault that causes the autopilot to disengage, will the warning be the same as when the autopilot is manually disconnected?

Same indications but either AP/SP DISC switch must be pressed to cancel the flashing AP—➤ on the PFD and the aural warning.

What conditions will cause the autopilot to automatically disengage?

- Wind shear
- Stall warning
- Failure of both YDs
- Wind shear avoidance procedures
- Unusual attitudes

Is the FD sync usable with the autopilot engaged?

No

What is the purpose of the button in the center of the course knob?

The button on the center of the course knob centers the HSI needle to the VOR station if it is being received.

If a new FD mode is selected and becomes active, what is the annunciation in the FMA?

For 5 seconds the new mode will flash green and then go steady.

What is happening when the AP XFR button on the FCP is activated?

The co-pilots FCC gives guidance to both FDs. The exception to this is during APPR, TO and GA modes when the FCC 1 and 2 are providing onside guidance.

chapter 3

Auxiliary Power Unit (APU)

What type of APU does the CRJ 700 have?

Allied Signal RE220RJ.

Where is the APU located?

The APU is located in the tail cone in a fireproof compartment.

What is the range of the APU exhaust hazard area?

There is none.

What fuel tank does the APU draw fuel from?

The left collector tank.

Where is the APU intake door located?

It is on the right side of the tail cone area.

What controls the position of the APU air inlet door?

The APU ECU controls the position of the APU air inlet door.

When will the APU door open during flight?

The APU door will open when the START/STOP switchlight is pressed. This is to prevent spin up from air flow.

What is the maximum operating altitude of the APU?

41,000 feet

What is the maximum altitude to start the APU?

37,000 feet

What is the maximum altitude to extract bleed air for air conditioning?

25,000 feet

What is the maximum altitude to use the APU for an in-flight engine start?

21,000 feet

Under a full load how much fuel does the APU burn?

The fuel burn is approximately 280 lbs. an hour.

Normally how is fuel supplied to the APU?

Pressurized fuel is supplied via a 28-VDC electric fuel pump.

What will happen if the APU fuel feed pump fails when the APU is operating?

The APU will still operate by getting fuel past the pump through an internal bypass valve.

What are the three methods to stop fuel flow to the APU?

- APU FIRE PUSH switchlight.
- The START/STOP switchlight on the APU panel.
- ECU automatic shutdown.

Does the EICAS APU door position correspond to the actual door position?

The EICAS only has two positions, open and closed. The APU door position does vary in flight with positions other than just open.

What is the limitation if the APU door is failed open and not operating, or the door position is not known?

The airspeed is restricted to 220 KIAS or the APU must remain operating

What is the primary purpose of the APU?

The primary purpose of the APU is to provide electrical power.

What is the KVA rating of the APU AC generator and up to what altitude will it provide this KVA?

Up to 41,000 feet the AC generator will provide 40 KVA.

What is the normal position of the APU generator switch?

For all normal operations the switch is to remain in AUTO.

What does the AVAIL light in the APU START/STOP switchlight indicate?

The APU is ready for electrical loading.

Can the APU be used for anti-icing bleed air?

No

Can the APU bleed air and another source of bleed air be used at the same time?

No

When does the bleed air source switch to and from the APU if operating?

Bleed air extraction will switch from the APU to the engines automatically when the TO bit is set. When the approach bit is set the bleed air source will switch back to the APU for landing.

What battery is needed to start the APU?

Both the MAIN and APU battery are needed to start and operate the APU.

What is the minimum required battery voltage required to start the APU?

22 volts

What happens when the APU PWR FUEL switchlight is pressed?

- The APU ECU is powered.
- The APU SOV OPEN status message appears.
- APU fuel pump activates.
- The APU IN BITE status message will be displayed until the APU door is open.
- APU EGT and RPM gauges display.
- After 10 seconds the APU DOOR OPEN message will appear. The APU door will not open in flight until the START/STOP switchlight is pressed to prevent the APU from wind milling.

At what point will the APU START status message disappear during an APU start?

Prior to 60% the START switchlight and APU START status message will disappear.

When will the APU AVAIL light illuminate?

When the APU is at 99% RPM + 2 seconds the APU AVAIL light will illuminate.

When will the APU ECU inhibit a start due to APU RPM?

The APU ECU will inhibit a start while on the ground if the RPM exceeds 5% or in flight if the RPM exceeds 12%.

How long would you wait after an APU start attempt before trying another start?

Wait two minutes for the starter motor and start contactor to cool and for fuel drainage.

When the APU START/STOP switchlight is pressed to turn off the APU what actually closes to shut off the fuel?

The fuel solenoid closes and not the SOV.

What are some of the conditions the APU will auto shutdown on the ground and in flight?

Shutdown Conditions	Ground	Flight
APU Fire	x	x
Loss of speed sensor signal or speed protection	x	x
Over-speed which is >106% RPM	x	x
APU door closes when APU operating or APU door fails to open	x	x
No rotation or no light-off	x	x
Failure of the ECU	x	x
Slow to start	x	x
No acceleration	x	x
RPM falls back after starter cutout	x	x
Loss of door position sensor signal	x	x
Loss of DC power	x	x
APU over temperature	x	Note 1
Failure of oil pressure switch or low oil pressure	x	Note 2
High oil temperature	x	Note 2
Under-speed of RPM	x	Note 2
Reverse flow (LCV)	x	Note 2
Loss of EGT sensor	x	Note 2
Impending bypass of APU oil filter	x	Note 2

Note 1: If an engine is being started using the APU, auto shutdown is inhibited until the starter disengages.

Note 2: Sixty seconds after landing the APU will enter ground mode and auto shutdown will occur.

How can the APU be shut down from outside the aircraft?

A switch is located on the external services panel that is located on the right forward part of the fuselage. Another cutoff switch is located in the APU compartment.

How is the APU SOV closed?

Automatically by the detection of a fire, manually when the APU FIRE PUSH or the PWR FUEL is pressed.

How is the APU SOV opened?

Pressing the PWR FUEL switch opens the APU SOV.

An APU has an overload condition with both electrical and pneumatic loads on. Which will the ECU give priority to, electrical or pneumatic?

The ECU will give priority to electrical requirements.

How does the pilot discharge the APU fire extinguisher if there is an APU fire on the ground?

The APU fire bottle will automatically discharge 5 seconds after the fire warning.

What aural warning is associated with an APU fire?

A fire bell in the cockpit will sound with an APU fire.

Explain the APU fire loops.

The APU has two fire loops in parallel around the APU. The loops are connected to the FIDEEX and monitored. Both loops must detect an overheat condition before annunciating an APU fire.

What would happen if an APU fire loop experienced an open circuit or short?

An APU FIRE FAIL caution message would be displayed on the EICAS. The FIDEEX would automatically monitor only the good loop.

What fire extinguishing agent is used to extinguish an APU fire?

Halon is used to extinguish an APU fire.

What does the START/STOP switchlight operate?

This switchlight operates the starter motor control circuit and energizes the start motor.

When does the APU starter motor disengage?

46% RPM when on the ground and 60 % RPM when in flight.

When does the APU ignition turn off during a start?

95 % RPM

During APU shutdown what does pressing the PWR/FUEL switchlight do after pressing the START/STOP switchlight?

The fuel SOV is closed and electrical power to the ECU is removed.

The battery master is ON and the PWR FUEL switchlight is pressed, what then occurs?

- The ECU is powered.
- APU IN BITE (self-test).
- APU fuel pump activates.
- APU RPM and EGT gauges appear.
- Fuel shutoff valve opens (APU SOV OPEN).
- APU air inlet door opens (DOOR OPEN).

What does the amber PUMP FAIL in the PWR FUEL switchlight indicate?

The APU fuel pump has failed.

What does the amber SOV FAIL in the PWR FUEL switchlight indicate?

This light indicates the APU fuel feed SOV has failed.

What will cause the APU FIRE PUSH switchlight to illuminate?

The detection of an APU fire will illuminate the switchlight.

What occurs when the APU FIRE PUSH switchlight is pressed?

- The APU shuts down.
- APU fuel pump is turned off.
- APU bleed air LCV closes.
- The squib on the APU bottle is armed.

What does a green BOTTLE ARMED PUSH TO DISCH switchlight indicate?

The bottle is charged and the squib is armed.

How could the APU manually be selected as the only bleed air source?

Set the BLEED VALVES selector to MANUAL. The BLEED SOURCE selector should be set to APU. Now the APU is the only source of bleed air. The ISOL valve can be opened to allow the APU to supply the left and right pneumatic systems.

What RPM is considered an APU over speed?

More than 106% RPM is an over speed condition and the APU will automatically shutdown.

How is bleed air reverse flow to the APU prevented?

The logic in the ACSCs and a one way check valve prevent reverse flow to the APU.

What controls the APU LCV?

The APU LCV can be controlled manually via the BLEED AIR panel or automatically by the APU ECU and ACSC.

What valve opens when the APU is providing electrical power above 17,000 feet?

The surge control valve (SCV) opens when the APU is supplying electrical power above 17,000 feet. The opening of this valve helps to reduce the chances of APU surges when it is operating in an unloaded bleed air condition.

Other than the SCV what valve also helps with surge and compressor stall protection?

The LCV helps with surge and compressor stall protection.

When is the APU ready for pneumatic loading?

In flight the ECU will not allow pneumatic loading until 2 seconds after the APU reaches 99% RPM. On the ground pneumatic loading will not occur for 60 seconds after 99% RPM.

What does an APU status message DOOR INHIB/CLSD or DOOR INHIB/OPEN indicate?

The APU inlet door is inhibited open or closed by maintenance.

What do amber dashes for a door position indicate?

The position of the APU door is not known.

Where does the APU cooling and ventilation air discharge?

The air discharges through the exhaust duct on the tail along with the APU exhaust.

chapter 4

Communications

What is the purpose of the backup-tuning unit?

In the event of an AC power loss or dual RTU failure, the back up tuning unit provides direct control of the NAV 1 and COM 1.

When does the CVR begin to record?

The CVR begins to record once the DC ESS bus is powered. Recording begins basically once the aircraft has power.

When does the FDR begin to record?

The FDR begins to record if either the strobes or beacon is turned on or the aircraft is weight-off-wheels.

When EMER is selected on the audio control panel (ACP) does the handheld microphone operate?

The handheld microphone is disabled.

How do you adjust the volume of the aural warning system?

It is not adjustable by the pilots because the aural warning system does not go through the volume control switches.

With the radio transmit (R/T) - intercom (I/C) switch in the I/C position, where can your intercom transmission be heard?

At all interior and exterior interphone units.

What is the purpose of the VOICE/BOTH switch?

BOTH allows the pilot to hear the Morse code and voice messages from the station. VOICE filters out the Morse code so only the voice message can be heard.

Where is the observer's overhead speaker located?

The observer seat does not have a speaker; therefore the observer's audio control panel speaker knob is inoperative.

Explain the EMER/NORM switch on the ACPs.

When there is a failure of the audio integrating system, the EMER position should be selected. This causes the electronic circuits of the audio integrating system to be bypassed and most of the ACP functions will be inoperative. If the pilot were to select EMER, his headset will be directly connected to NAV 1 and VHF 1. The aural warning system will be operable. Basically this switch directly connects communication, navigation and the aural warning system.

If the co-pilot selects EMER, his headset is connected directly to NAV 2 and VHF 2. All ACP services are lost except for NAV 2 and VHF 2.

The switch on the observer's ACP is disabled.

Explain the public address system (PA) priority?

1. Pilots
2. FA

- Pilots can override the FAs PA.

How is the speaker volume in the cabin, lavatory and galley adjusted?

It is adjusted automatically based on the background noise. It is at full volume when the APU or an engine is running.

What could be the problem if the FA said the speaker in the galley was not working when he made a PA?

The galley speaker does not work when a PA is made from the FA's station.

Explain the interphone control unit.

The interphone control unit is located on the center pedestal and has four switchlights: PA, CHIME, CALL, and EMERG. Only one mode can be selected at one time.

How would you make a PA to the cabin?

The ACP transmit switch should be selected to PA, and then press the PA switchlight. The R/T switch on the control wheel, the ACP R/T switch or the handheld microphone can be used to make the PA. When finished, move the ACP switch from PA to another position to turn it off.

What occurs when the CALL switchlight is pressed?

The switchlight illuminates green and there is an aural high-low chime. A red light illuminates on the overhead exit sign in the middle of the cabin and the FLT light illuminates green on the FA's handset cradle.

Explain the EMER switchlight on the interphone control unit.

It is used to notify the FA of an emergency condition. When pressed the switchlight flashes amber and there is an aural high-low chime. There will be a red flashing light on the mid-cabin overhead exit sign and the amber EMG light flashes on the FA's handset cradle.

When the FA calls the flight deck, what should be selected to activate communications?

Select PA on the ACP mic selector switch.

At what locations can maintenance use the interphone system to talk with the pilots?

- Avionics bay
- Aft equipment bay
- Refuel/defuel control panel
- External service panel

Explain the MECH PUSH switchlight.

This is a call function between the flight deck and the external service panel and the aft equipment bay. There is a switchlight on the three panels will illuminate when one switch is pressed. It will be accompanied with an aural tone in the cabin. The lights remain on for 30 seconds.

What is the purpose of the backup tuning unit?

This radio provides control of COM 1 and NAV 1 in the event of complete loss of AC power or both radio-tuning units (RTU) fail. COM 1, NAV 1 and the backup-tuning unit are powered from the battery bus.

What system controls are available on the RTUs?

- VHF communication radios
- VHF navigation radios
- TCAS
- Transponders
- ADF
- Optional HF radio

Explain the two pages of the RTUs.

The RTU has a top page and a main page. The top page allows basic changes to the VHF radios, transponder, ADF and the main page is dedicated to a specific navigation, TCAS or communication system. Pressing the associated button twice activates main page.

Example: Press the RTU TCAS button twice to access the TCAS main page.

Explain the 1/2 button on the RTU.

This button is the RTU cross-side tuning button. The RTUs are normally set up for on-side control of the radios. The 1/2 key allows one RTU to display and control the other side.

Cross-side information is in yellow. Pushing the 1/2 key a second time will return the radio to a normal on-side display. This feature is used when an RTU fails but the radio and navigation functions still work.

If an RTU fails, what would it look like and what should the pilot do?

The display would be blank and cross-side tuning would be inoperative. Cross-side tuning needs to be established. Inhibit the failed RTU by selecting the RTU INHIBIT switch for the failed RTU. Cross-side tuning is now available and can be activated by pressing the 1/2 on the serviceable RTU.

Both radios are available but cannot be shown on one RTU at the same time. The 1/2 button achieves switching between the two radios.

Explain the STBY position of the backup tuning unit.

In this position the backup tuning unit is in standby. The frequencies will duplicate COM 1 and NAV 1 frequencies.

When would you use the backup tuning unit?

When both RTUs and the FMS fail or there is a complete loss of AC power.

Besides the RTUs and the backup tuning unit, where can the radio frequencies be changed?

On the FMS radio tuning page.

Explain the FMS TUNE INHIBIT switch.

When in the INHIBIT position, the remote tuning function of the FMS is inhibited. This may be needed if the remote FMS control malfunctions.

Where is the cockpit voice recorder (CVR) located?

The CVR is located in the tail section of the airplane.

What four locations are recorded on the CVR?

- Pilot station
- Copilot station
- Area microphone in the cockpit
- Mixed PA audio and the observer station

How long does the CVR record?

The time is 120 minutes and at the end of the cycle it will re-record.

When does the CVR start recording?

The CVR begins recording when electrical power is applied to the aircraft.

Explain the CVR test button.

When pressed it completes an internal test of the CVR system. To test; hold the button for 5 seconds and a successful test is indicated by illumination of the green light in the button during the 5 seconds.

What is the function of the headset jack on the CVR control panel?

The headset jack is used to monitor the recording tone during the test.

Where is the flight data recorder unit (FDR) located?

The FDR is located in the tail section of the aircraft.

What does the FDR record and for how many hours?

It records the last 25 hours of aircraft and flight parameter data.

When does the FDR start recording?

When one of the following three occurs:

- Beacon is ON
- Strobes are ON
- Weight off wheels

What is the purpose of the FDR EVENT switch?

This will highlight an event on the FDR. The highlight is accomplished by pressing the FDR EVENT switch for 2 seconds, which will then display a green FDR EVENT advisory status message.

chapter 5

Doors

How many doors does the CRJ700 have?

There are a total of 9 doors and hatches.

- Avionics bay door
- Passenger door
- Flight deck escape hatch
- Galley service door
- Left overwing emergency exit
- Right overwing emergency exit
- Aft cargo bay
- Forward cargo bay
- Aft equipment bay

The proximity sensing electronic unit (PSEU) monitors which doors?

All except the overhead escape hatch in the cockpit and the aft equipment bay door.

- Passenger door
- Galley service door
- Two over wing emergency exits
- Avionics bay door
- Forward and aft cargo doors

What type of door is the forward cargo door?

This door is a semi-plug type door.

Is there any ventilation once the forward cargo door is closed?

Once equalized there is no ventilation in the forward cargo compartment.

How do you confirm the galley door is closed?

A green indicator below the inside handle.

What doors are available for emergency evacuation on the ground?

- Passenger door
- Service door
- Left and right over wing emergency exit
- Overhead escape hatch in the cockpit

What is the maximum door load?

The maximum door load is 1,000 lbs. or 4 passengers on the door at any one time.

Where is the avionics bay door?

The avionics bay door is on the bottom of the forward fuselage.

Is the aft equipment bay pressurized?

No

Can the overhead escape hatch be opened from the outside?

Yes

What indicates the overhead escape latch is properly secured?

The two green indicator pins will align with the alignment marks when it is secure.

Can the over wing exits be opened from the outside?

Yes

The over wing emergency exits look identical, can they be switched?

No

What does the EICAS message PASSENGER DOOR indicate?

The passenger door is unsafe and not completely locked and secured.

What are the closed and locked indications on the passenger door?

- The green marks in the indicator windows align with the marks on the latch pins. There are a total of four.

- The two locations for the latch cams align.

- A green LOCKED indication is displayed.

CRJ700

chapter 6

Electrical System

What are the sources of AC electrical power for the aircraft?

- The primary sources of AC electrical power are two engine driven integrated drive generators (IDGs).

- The APU has an AC generator mounted on it.

- An air driven generator (ADG) can provide AC power if there is a total loss of AC power.

- On the forward right side of the fuselage there is a receptacle for AC ground power.

What provides power if there is a total loss of AC electrical power in flight?

On the right side of the forward fuselage is an air driven generator (ADG) that can be deployed to provide AC power.

What is the kilo volt-amperes (KVA) rating of the integrated drive generators (IDG)?

The IDG rating is 40 KVA up to 41,000 feet.

What type of power do the IDGs supply?

The IDGs supply 115-volt AC, 400-hertz 3-phase electrical power.

Does the IDG RPM vary with engine RPM?

No, the generator must turn at a constant RPM to produce a steady 400-Hz. The constant speed drive (CSD) unit accomplishes this task.

How does the CSD accomplish a constant RPM?

The CSD is a hydro-mechanical unit and uses an integral oil system to drive the generator at a constant RPM. The CSD is driven by the engine accessory gearbox, which turns at a variable speed based on engine speed.

How is the internal oil of the CSD cooled?

The oil in the CSD is cooled by an air/oil heat exchanger. The air used to cool the oil is from the N1 fan.

How many batteries does the aircraft have?

The aircraft has two nicad batteries. One is located in the nose and one in the aft equipment bay.

What are the AC buses?

- AC service bus
- AC essential bus
- AC bus 1
- AC bus 2

What are the different ways the IDG can disconnect from the engine gearbox?

- Pressing the associated IDG DISC switch.
- When CSD internal temperature raises to a certain temperature the IDG will automatically disconnect.
- An over torque condition of the CSD will cause the shearing of the IDG drive shaft.

What does the white DISC in the IDG switchlight indicate?

The IDG was successfully disconnected from the engine accessory drive.

When will the engine generator automatically be tripped off line and removed from the bus system?

When any of the following occur:

- Generator or bus over current

- Over or under frequency

- Over or under voltage

What monitors the generator system?

Each generator has a generator control unit (GCU) that controls and monitors the related generator system. The GCU provides protection and voltage regulation for the associated generator.

What does the FAULT light in the IDG switchlight indicate?

This light will illuminate when the IDG oil overheats or oil pressure drops below limits. This FAULT light will also illuminate an IDG caution message on the EICAS.

Where is the external AC receptacle located?

The external AC connection is on the forward right side of the fuselage.

What does the green AVAIL light on the flight deck electrical power services control panel and the external service panel indicate?

When external AC power is attached to the aircraft, the external monitor checks the AC ground power for proper voltage, frequency, and phase relationship. If it is good power and available for use these two AVAIL lights will illuminate.

There is external AC power supplying the aircraft power, what will happen if an engine generator is selected on?

The buses will be supplied AC power from the engine generator and no longer from the AC external power. The green AVAIL lamp on the electrical control panel will illuminate and the white IN USE will extinguish, even if the switchlight is still selected in.

What occurs when the AC switchlight on the flight deck electrical power services panel has the green AVAIL light illuminated and is pressed?

If there is no other AC electrical power available, the external AC power will supply power. The white IN USE of the switchlight will illuminate and the green AVAIL will extinguish.

What buses are powered when external AC power is connected and the green AVAIL switchlight on the external services panel is pressed?

Only the AC service bus will be powered.

Explain a SERVICE CONFIGURATION message?

The AVAIL switchlight on the external AC service panel is activated and AC external power is connected.

What other bus does AC BUS 1 supply power to?

Normally to the AC ESS BUS.

Which other buses does AC BUS 2 supply power to?

Normally to AC SERV BUS.

What bus normally powers the AC ESS BUS and what would happen if there was a fault with this bus?

AC BUS 1 normally powers the AC ESS BUS. If AC BUS 1 fails, the ESS BUS will automatically transfer to AC BUS 2 for a power source.

If AC BUS 1 fails, what would you do if the ESS BUS did not automatically transfer to AC BUS 2?

The ESS BUS could be manually transferred to AC BUS 2 by the AC ESS XFER switchlight on the electrical power services panel. This will cause the AC ESS XFER switchlight to illuminate white and there will be a white status message AC ESS ALTN on the status page. This electrically connects the ESS BUS to AC BUS 2.

Will the AC ESS XFER switchlight illuminate if pressed for manual transfer?

Yes

After selecting the battery master to ON with no other power source, what does an illuminated AC ESS XFER switchlight indicate?

The AC ESS is not power by AC BUS 1. At this point neither AC BUS 1 nor 2 are powering the AC ESS BUS.

What would occur to the AC ESS BUS if total AC power were lost in flight?

The air driven generator (ADG) would automatically deploy and the AC ESS BUS would be powered. The ADG BUS is powered by the ADG and this bus is connected to the AC ESS BUS.

Aircraft generator power is re-established after a total AC power loss and ADG deployment. Will the aircraft generator now power the AC ESS BUS?

To de-energize the relay between the AC ESS BUS and the ADG BUS, the PWR TXFR OVERRIDE button on the ADG AUTO DEPLOY CONTROL panel must be pressed. This will connect the AC ESS BUS to AC BUS 1.

What bus powers the AC SERV BUS?

The AC BUS 2 supplies 115-volts AC to the AC service bus.

What does the AC ESS BUS power?

It powers equipment essential for flight and powers ESS TRU 1.

The cleaning crew needs to clean the aircraft, how would you power only the buses needed for cleaning?

External power available: If the AVAIL lamp in the EXT AC PUSH switchlight on the external services panel is illuminated, the switchlight can be pressed and if no other AC power is available to the aircraft, the AC SERV BUS will be powered with no other buses being powered.

What is the bus priority for AC BUS 1?

1. GEN 1

2. APU generator

3. GEN 2

4. External power

What is the bus priority for AC BUS 2?

1. GEN 2

2. APU generator

3. GEN 1

4. External power

What is the purpose of the bus priority system?

It is the automatic fault protection and transfer system of the AC electrical system. AC BUS 1 and AC BUS 2 are important buses and the bus priority ensures that these buses will be powered.

Example: Generator 1 normally powers AC BUS 1. If there is a fault in generator 1, AC BUS 1 will then transfer to the APU generator. If the APU is not available, it will transfer to generator 2. If generator 2 is not available it will look for external power.

What happens when AC BUS 1 has a short and takes generator 1 off line?

The bus priority system will have AC BUS 1 try to receive power from APU generator, generator 2, then external power in that order. This could take all the generators off line. The auto transfer inhibit will stop the transfer and an amber FAIL light in the AUTO XFER switchlight will illuminate. The FAIL means if has done its job. FAIL really means auto transfer inhibit of priority logic.

What does the white OFF in the AUTO XFER switchlights indicate?

This light will illuminate when the switchlight is pressed. When OFF is activated, auto transfer of AC BUS 1 or AC BUS 2 to another power source, depending on which is selected is inhibited.

What are the volts, Hz and KVA provided by the ADG?

The ADG provides 115 volts, 400 Hz, 15 KVA.

Where is the ADG located?

The ADG is located next to the nose gear on the forward right fuselage.

After deployment of the ADG in flight, how can it be retracted?

It can only be retracted on the ground.

What are the general components of the ADG?

It has an AC generator and a variable pitch two-bladed propeller.

Can the ADG automatically be deployed on the ground?

Weight on wheels (WOW) as sensed by the PSEU will not allow auto deployment.

What conditions will cause automatic deployment of the ADG in flight?

The ADG will automatically deploy with a complete AC power failure. The conditions that must be met are the battery master is ON, generators are inoperative and the main buses which are AC BUS 1 and 2 have lost power.

What will the ADG supply power to when it deploys with all other AC power sources inoperative in flight?

The ADG BUS powers the AC ESS BUS and the ACMP 3B hydraulic pump. The AC ESS BUS then powers the ESS TRU 1, DC ESS BUS, and the BATT BUS. The flaps, slats and pitch trim channel 2 will operate.

Explain the PWR TXFR OVERRIDE switch?

After ADG deployment it may be possible to get an aircraft generator on line. The generator would then be powering most of the AC buses and the PWR TXFR OVERRIDE switch would transfer the AC ESS BUS to the aircraft generator. It would also transfer the hydraulic pump ACMP 3B from the ADG BUS to the normal AC power source.

What is required for the EMER PWR ONLY message to display on the EICAS?

EMER PWR ONLY message displays when the AC ESS BUS and the ADG BUS are connected by the ADG essential relay. This occurs when the ADG is deployed and the propeller rotates to generate power to energize the AC essential relay.

As the ADG propeller rotates it generates power to close two relays. What are the relays?

The hydraulic pump transfer relay and the AC essential relay.

What is the maximum speed for ADG operation?

Vmo/Mmo

When is the ADG bus displayed?

The ADG bus is displayed when the ADG is deployed.

When will the ADG volts and frequency display on the AC electrical page?

The volts and frequency readings will display in a box above the ADG bus when ADG voltage is greater than 10 volts and the frequency is more than 300 Hz.

What could be done if auto deployment of the ADG did not occur with the failure of all AC power in flight?

Pulling the ADG manual-deploy handle at the bottom of the center pedestal would manually deploy the ADG. Deployment will be indicated by an ADG shown on the ELEC synoptic page, and EMER PWR ONLY EICAS message.

Explain the LAMP/UNIT switch on the ADG AUTO DEPLOY CONTROL panel.

- LAMP position: This checks the light bulb on the AUTO DEPLOY CONTROL unit.

- UNIT position: AC BUS 1 and 2 must be powered and two generators operating for an accurate test. In the TEST position the control unit will check the logic circuit of the control unit and the transfer relay.

After ADG deployment, an engine generator is brought on line. You press the power transfer override switch to return the ESS BUS and hydraulic 3B to normal AC power but nothing happens. What could cause this?

The ADG manual-deploy handle needs to be stowed for this to work.

Why does the checklist require the ADG manual deploy handle to remain pulled out?

If it is pushed back in, with the weight on wheels signal at touchdown the emergency tie contactors will receive this signal and the battery power will be removed from the DC ESS BUS.

At about 80 knots the ADG will not be providing power and the only power left is the battery which will power the DC ESS BUS only if the ADG handle is pulled.

What are the nine DC buses?

- DC BUS 1 (main)
- DC BUS 2 (main)
- DC ESS BUS (essential)
- DC SERV BUS (service)
- DC UTIL BUS (utility)
- DC BATT BUS (battery)
- MAIN BATT DIR BUS (battery direct)
- APU BATT DIR BUS (battery direct)
- DC EMER BUS (emergency)

What are the four TRUs and their power source?

- ESS TRU 1 – AC ESS BUS
- ESS TRU 2 – AC BUS 2
- TRU 1 – AC BUS 1
- TRU 2 – AC BUS 2

What is considered the emergency DC power?

The batteries are considered emergency DC power.

What produces DC power?

DC power is produced by 4 TRUs and two batteries. The TRUs convert AC power to DC power.

Explain the DC power centers (DCPC).

Two DCPCs are part of the DC power system and control distribution of DC power. The DC tie contractors are automatically operated during malfunctions by the DCPC to provide power to as many buses as possible.

When the main DC tie closes what bus is shed?

The DC UTIL BUS sheds.

Explain the primary batteries of the aircraft.

The main battery is located in the nose area and the APU battery is located in the aft equipment bay. Both are nickel-cadmium (nicad) batteries. The APU battery is a 24 volt 43 ampere/hour and the main battery is 24 volt 17 ampere/hour

What does the DC UTIL BUS power?

The passenger service unit reading lights are powered by the DC UTIL BUS.

What is load-shed when either TRU 1 or TRU 2 fail?

The DC UTIL BUS is load-shed.

Where is the DC external power receptacle located?

No DC external power receptacle is installed.

How do the TRUs provide DC power?

The TRUs provide 28 volt DC by transforming and rectifying the supplied 115-volt AC electrical power.

What is the amp rating of the TRUs?

120 amps

What are the four TRUs?

- TRU 1
- TRU 2
- ESS (essential) TRU 1
- ESS (essential) TRU 2

What does the main battery provide power to?

- Flight deck lighting system.
- Backup power to the clocks and data concentrator units (DCUs).
- Backup power to the AHRS, APU electronic control unit (ECU) and the proximity sensor electronic unit (PSEU).

What does the APU battery provide power to?

- Power to start the APU
- DC EMER BUS
- APU BATT DIR BUS
- MAIN BATT DIR BUS
- DC BATT BUS

What buses are the battery chargers located on?

- AC BUS 1 powers the main battery charger.
- The AC service bus powers the APU battery charger.

What happens to the APU battery and the main battery during a complete AC power failure (APU GEN, GEN 1, GEN 2 failure)?

The two batteries are bridged.

What TIE closes during a complete AC power failure?

The ESS TIE closes to connect the battery bus to the DC ESS BUS for emergency power.

What TIE closes if TRU 1 or TRU 2 fails?

The MAIN TIE will close to connect the operating TRU to DC BUS 1 and DC BUS 2.

What bus is shed when the MAIN TIE closes?

The DC UTIL BUS will shed to reduce the load on the TRUs.

When will the CROSS TIE close?

The CROSS TIE will close when both TRU 1 and TRU 2 fail or both ESS TRUs fail.

If the AC BUS 2 fails what will power ESS TRU 2?

The ESS TRU 2 will be powered by the AC ESS BUS after an AC BUS 2 failure.

What buses are powered with emergency DC power?

- DC BATT BUS
- EMERGENCY BUS
- DC ESS BUS

What bus is powered when the DC service switch is in the ON position?

The DC SERV BUS is powered by the APU battery direct bus.

What does the DC service switch on the flight deck electrical panel do?

The DC service switch powers the DC SERV BUS for servicing the aircraft.

What does the DC SERV BUS supply power to?

The external navigation lights including the beacon and lighting in the passenger cabin.

What does the DC UTIL BUS power?

The DC UTIL BUS powers the passenger service unit reading lights.

When the MAIN TIE closes what is load shed?

The DC UTIL BUS is load shed.

During emergency power conditions what three buses are powered by the main battery and the APU battery?

- DC ESS BUS
- Emergency DC bus
- DC BATT BUS

What buses do the batteries directly power?

The main battery directly powers the MAIN BATT DIR BUS and the APU battery powers the APU BATT DIR BUS.

Why is the DC emergency bus (DC EMER BUS) not depicted on the DC electrical page?

It will be displayed only when the bus is not powered or has a fault.

Explain the DC EMER BUS?

This bus is connected to the APU DIR BATT BUS and the BATT BUS, which means it is continuously powered. This bus provides power to the following:

- Left and right engine fuel SOVs.
- APU fuel SOV.
- The number 1 fire extinguisher for the left and right engine.
- The number 2 fire extinguisher for the left and right engine.
- APU battery direct bus feed.
- Hydraulic SOVs for the left and right engines.

While in flight with the main and APU batteries the only source of power, how long will they provide power?

Approximately 30 minutes

Basically what does the BATTERY MASTER switch do in the ON position?

The APU battery and the main battery are connected to their respective battery buses.

What does the half intensity magenta color usually indicate?

This color logic for this color indicates invalid data or insufficient data.

What are the sources of DC electrical power?

- Four transformer rectifier units (TRUs)
- Two nickel cadmium (nicad) batteries

If all TRUs failed would the DC ESS BUS be powered?

The DC ESS BUS would be powered by the APU and the MAIN BATT DIR BUS.

Would the DC ESS BUS be powered if both ESS TRU 1 and 2 failed?

The DC ESS BUS would still be powered through the CROSS TIE.

Fire and Overheat Protection

What areas do the fire detection and extinguishing (FIDEEX) monitor?

- Engine

- Main landing gear

- APU

- Cargo compartments

Where does the FIDEEX unit provide fire extinguishing?

- APU

- Cargo compartments

- Engine

What does the FIDEEX control?

- Smoke detection

- Overheat detection

- Fire protection system

- Fire extinguishing systems

What areas have smoke detection systems?

- The two cargo bays

- The two lavatorys

What compartments provide fire and overheat detection?

The APU and the engine have fire and overheat detection.

What area only has overheat protection?

The main landing gear bays only have overheat detection.

What in the engine actually detects the fire or overheat condition?

Two detection loops that are connected to FIDEEX detect the fire or overheat condition. As there is an increase in temperature i.e. fire, the electrical resistance of the insulator decreases with an increase in temperature to a trip point at which there will be a fire or overheat indication generated.

What are the two benefits of the dual loop detection systems?

- Minimize false fire warnings because both loops must sense the fire or overheat condition before a fire is detected.

- The aircraft can be dispatched with a loop that is inoperative and still provide fire and overheat protection.

Explain the operation of the fire detection control unit.

This unit monitors the electrical resistance of the loops. Both loops must sense the same decrease in electrical resistance at the same time for the fire detection control unit to send the signal to the EICAS. This unit also monitors the loops for malfunctions and if a malfunction is detected in a loop, the second loop maintains the capability of detecting an overheat condition or fire. The failed loop will no longer be used.

What do the engine fire extinguisher bottles contain?

The bottles contain Halon and are pressurized with nitrogen.

Where are the engine fire extinguishers located?

The extinguishers are located in the aft equipment bay.

Will the left engine fire bottle only discharge into the left engine?

No, both bottles can be discharged into a single engine. This is determined by which fire switch is pressed. Both bottles have a left and right squib that allows the bottle contents to be used in either engine.

What happens when the LH or RH FIRE PUSH switchlight is pressed?

- Fuel SOV closes.

- Bleed air SOV is closed.

- Hydraulic SOV is closed.

- Engine driven generator is taken off line.

- Squibs on both engine fire extinguishing bottles arm. Both BOTTLE ARMED PUSH TO DISCH switchlights illuminate.

What is indicated by the BOTTLE 1 and 2 ARMED PUSH TO DISCH switchlights being illuminated after pressing a LH or RH FIRE PUSH switchlight?

When illuminated it indicates the squib is armed and charged.

What does an illuminated BOTTLE 1 and 2 ARMED PUSH TO DISCH switchlight during the test of the fire warning system?

The applicable squib will operate normal.

What will happen if a LH or RH FIRE PUSH switchlight is pressed out after activating the switchlight?

The systems affected by pressing the switchlight the first time will return to normal operation and fire alerting is returned to normal.

What happens when a BOTTLE ARMED PUSH TO DISCH switchlight is pressed after being activated by the FIRE switchlight?

An electrical current fires the squib on the selected bottle. The Halon is directed into the engine nacelle on the side of the selected fire switch.

What determines which engine nacelle the fire extinguisher bottle will be discharged into?

The engine nacelle is determined by which FIRE PUSH switchlight is pressed.

How many loops are used to detect a fire or overheat condition of the APU?

Two loops of the same design as the engine loops.

What monitors the fire loops of the APU?

The FIDEEX unit monitors the fire loops of the APU.

Explain the two modes of operation of the APU fire detection?

- Ground: When there is a fire condition with the aircraft on the ground, the APU will shut down automatically. Five seconds after shut down, the APU fire bottle discharges into the APU enclosure automatically.

- Flight: When a fire is detected the APU will automatically shut down. The Halon will not discharge automatically, the crew must do it.

How many squibs does the APU fire bottle have?

Two

Where is the APU fire detection loops located?

The loops are around the inside of the APU enclosure.

What aural warning is associated with an APU fire?

A fire bell on the flight deck will sound with an APU fire.

Explain the APU fire loops.

The APU has two fire loops in parallel around the APU. The loops are connected to the FIDEEX and monitored. Both loops must detect an overheat condition before annunciating an APU fire.

What will happen if an APU fire loop has an open circuit or short?

An APU FIRE FAIL caution message will be displayed on the EICAS and the FIDEEX will automatically monitor only the good loop.

Where is the fire extinguisher bottle for the APU located?

It is located in the aft equipment bay.

What happens when the APU FIRE PUSH switchlight is pressed?

- APU fuel feed SOV is closed.

- APU is shutdown by closing the fuel solenoid valve.

- APU LCV is closed.

- APU generator is taken off line.

- Both squibs are armed and the BOTTLE ARMED PUSH TO DISCH switchlight is illuminated.

What happens when the APU BOTTLE ARMED PUSH TO DISCH switchlight is pressed after it is activated?

When pressed, an electrical current fires the two squibs and pressurized Halon is released into the APU enclosure.

Explain the Halon extinguishing system for the cargo compartments.

The system has two bottles that are shared between the FWD and AFT cargo compartments. One bottle discharges immediately and the other over an extended period of time.

How many cargo fire detectors are installed?

Two fire detectors are installed in the aft cargo and three in the forward cargo.

How many cargo smoke detectors need to detect smoke to activate the warning?

One of the two in the aft and two of the three in the forward need to detect smoke to activate the SMOKE FWD (AFT) CARGO message.

What happens when an illuminated FWD or AFT red CARGO SMOKE PUSH switchlight is pressed?

Pressing the FWD or AFT CARGO SMOKE PUSH switchlight arms the forward or aft squibs on the bottles. The BOTTLE ARMED PUSH TO DISCHARGE switchlight will illuminate. If the AFT CARGO SMOKE PUSH is selected it will shut off the cargo heater and close the intake and exhaust SOV.

Where are the cargo HALON extinguishers located?

Both cargo extinguishers are in the aft corner of the right wing box.

How is the discharge of the cargo extinguisher bottle accomplished?

By pressing the illuminated BOTTLE ARMED PUSH TO DISCHARGE the squibs will discharge the Halon to the appropriate cargo bin.

How many squibs does each cargo extinguishing bottle have?

2 each

What is the difference between the cargo fire extinguisher bottles?

They discharge the Halon at different rates. The squibs fire at the same time but one bottle discharges the Halon immediately and the other bottle discharges the Halon slowly. The purpose of the second bottle discharging slowly is to maintain a presence of Halon for about 60 minutes.

Are the smoke detectors susceptible to false alarms?

Mobile radios or cell phones on the ground near the detectors or exhaust from equipment can set them off.

Where is the smoke detector located in the lavatory?

The smoke detector is located on the ceiling.

When the lavatory smoke detector detects smoke, what happens?

SMOKE FWD or AFT LAV will be displayed on the primary page of the EICAS and an alarm on the detector will sound.

What happens when the lavatory smoke detector is tested by pressing the self-test switch on the detector?

- The detector will sound an alarm.

- A red light on the detector will illuminate

- The EICAS will display a SMOKE FWD (AFT) LAV.

- If the systems are operable the advisory FIRE SYS OK will be displayed.

What indicates the lavatory smoke detector is powered?

A green indicator light on the detector indicates it is powered.

How is a lavatory smoke detector reset?

A button on the smoke detector can reset the detector. This will cancel the visual and aural alarms. If smoke is still present after the reset the alarm will resume when the button is released.

Do the lavatories have any type of fire extinguishing?

Fire extinguishing is only provided in the waste bin.

Explain the fire extinguisher in the waste bin.

Two heat sensitive plugs melt and release the Halon into the bin. The fire extinguisher bottle is located on a bracket beside the waste bin.

Where is the fire extinguisher located on the flight deck?

The fire extinguisher is located behind the co-pilot's seat. It is a Halon fire extinguisher.

Are fire extinguishers located in the cabin?

Two Halon fire extinguishers (one aft and one forward) are located in the cabin. A portable water extinguisher may also be in the cabin.

What detects an overheat condition in the main landing gear bay?

A single detection loop in the top of each wheel bin that is monitored by the overheat detection unit.

How does the loop in the landing gear bay detect an overheat condition?

The loop has an outer metal cover with two internal wires separated by insulating material. As heat is increased the resistance of the insulator decreases. At a certain point a signal will be sent to the monitor and a overheat indication will be displayed.

How is a main landing gear bay overheat brought to the pilots attention?

A MLG BAY OVHT warning message will be displayed on the EICAS and an aural alert will sound, "gear bay overheat".

What will happen if the gear bay overheat detection loop fails?

The control unit continuously monitors the loop and if the loop is not working properly, an amber EICAS message MLG OVHT FAIL is displayed on the EICAS.

Explain the MLG BAY OVHT switch on the landing gear control panel.

When held in the OVHT position, a simulated overheat condition in the main landing gear bay will be indicated by a red MLG BAY OVHT warning message with an aural alert "gear bay overheat".

Explain the OVHT TEST WARN FAIL switch on the landing gear control panel.

This switch will simulate the failure of the main landing gear bay overheat detection system. This test will generate an amber MLG OVHT FAIL caution message.

How is the FIDEEX system tested?

Press the test switch on the FIRE DETECTION FIREX MONITOR panel. This is an automated test and a good test is indicated by a FIRE SYS OK advisory message. All switchlights associated with the fire zones along with the master warnings will illuminate.

What is tested when the FIDEEX test button is pressed?

The areas tested with this button are the APU and engine detection systems along with the cargo extinguishing and smoke detector systems.

After pressing the FIRE DETECTION FIREX MONITOR TEST button what would indicate a problem with a system?

If a FIRE FAIL caution message is present there is a failure of that system. If there is a FAULT STATUS message then there is a loss of redundancy of that system

When the FWD or AFT CARGO SMOKE PUSH switchlight is pressed in, what is this actually doing?

All of the squibs on the two cargo bottles are armed. The BOTLE ARMED PUSH TO DISCH switchlight will illuminate due to the squibs being armed. The AFT switchlight will also turn off the heater and closes the air conditioning SOV.

How can the fire bell on the flight deck be silenced?

The fire bell can be silenced by pressing the master warning switchlight.

Does the jet pipe area have overheat detection?

This is part of the engine fire detection.

What part of the engine is provided fire extinguishing by the Halon?

Engine core area

chapter 8

Flight Controls

What do the multifunction spoilers (MFS) do?

The MFS are flight spoilers that provide roll control.

How many MFS are installed?

Two MFS are on each wing, an inboard and outboard for a total of four.

What drives the MFS panel?

One PDU and one hydraulic system power a MFS panel. This is so that a failure of a single hydraulic system will allow at least one panel on each wing to still operate.

During a turn will both MFS panels on the down wing operate?

During slower speeds both MFS panels operate if necessary.

What panels extend when the flight spoilers are selected?

All four MFS panels will extend when the flight spoilers are selected.

What controls the MFS operation?

Spoiler stabilizer control units (SSCU 1, SSCU 2) control the MFS panels. The deflection angles are determined by various aircraft systems inputs.

Describe the rudder travel limiter (RTL)?

The RTL limits the rudder travel during flight. There is still plenty of rudder travel to control the aircraft but the purpose is to prevent overstressing of the vertical stabilizer. As aircraft speed increases the rudder travel is gradually decreased from 33° to 4° to either side by the spoiler and stabilizer control units (SSCUs). Flap position is also one of the conditions that determine RTL.

What factors determine the maximum rudder travel limit?

The rudder travel limit is a function of airspeed, weight off wheels signal, flap selection and the number of engines operating.

What indications do the pilots have in reference to the rudder limit position?

On the flight control synoptic page there are two vertical bars that move to show the RTL.

What is the green range of the stabilizer trim?

3.5 to 11.5.

How many slat panels are on each wing?

3

How are the slats controlled?

The slats are controlled by selection of the SLATS/FLAPS lever and the slat flap electronic control unit (SFECU) controls the movement. Electric motors, gearbox, torque tubes and mechanical actuators move the slats. Electric brakes on the PDUs and the outer portions of the torque tubes hold the selected position of the slats.

What would happen if a problem were detected during slat extension?

The brakes would stop slat movement.

When is flap setting of 1 used?

This setting extends the slats to 20 degrees with no flaps extend. This is only used during retraction of slats and flaps after takeoff or go around.

What are the two positions of the slats?

The two positions are 20 and 25 degrees.

When do the slats extend and retract in relation to the flaps?

The slats are first during extension and last during retraction.

What is the purpose of the emergency flap switch?

In the event of a failure of the SLATS/FLAP lever, the emergency flap switch provides limited flap selection.

What happens when the emergency flap switch is selected to DEPLOY?

The SFECU will fully extend the slats and the flaps to 20 degrees.

Can the DEPLOY position of the emergency flap switch be selected at any speed?

Above 230 knots the switch is inhibited. You can select it but it won't do anything.

What happens if after selection of the emergency flap switch to deploy, the pilot returned the switch to normal?

In flight the flaps and slats will return to the position of the SLAT/FLAP lever.

Explain the spoiler/stab test (SPOST).

Upon first powering up the aircraft the SPOST1 test is automatically run after certain conditions are met. After both channels of the stab trim are engaged and all three hydraulic systems are powered the SPOST2 test begins. During the SPOST test there is a SPLR/STAB IN TEST advisory message and all flight control systems should not be moved and are inoperative. After the test, the message will disappear with no fault messages if it was a good test.

Explain how the aileron control system is actually two separate systems.

The pilot controls the left aileron and the co-pilot controls the right aileron. Under normal operations the aileron controls are interconnected with coordinated movement of the control surfaces.

What happens if an aileron PCU causes an un-commanded roll, with a runaway aileron?

A bungee breakout switch with the aileron system that is running away sends a signal to the SSCU. The SSCU then will command the MFS to respond to control wheel inputs and will present on the EICAS a PLT ROLL CMD or CPLT ROLL CMD. The SSCU will also illuminate the green PLT ROLL or CPLT ROLL switchlight on the glare shield in front of the pilot that should take control prior to ordering the ROLL DISC handle to be pulled.

What does a PLT or CPLT ROLL CMD advisory message indicate?

This message indicates the aileron circuit that has flight spoiler control.

What keeps the aileron control surface from fluttering in flight if all hydraulic pressure is lost to a PCU?

Each aileron has a flutter damper to prevent flutter.

Do all of the aileron PCUs need to be working for the aileron trim to work properly?

Minimum of one out of three PCUs needs to be operative. Hydraulic power from one of three systems is needed to adjust aileron trim.

Explain how aileron trim is accomplished?

Both switches of the AIL TRIM must be pushed left or right to actuate the aileron trim. When the switch is actuated, signals are sent to reposition the aileron cables; this will cause the control wheels to move.

What is the color of the neutral position of the aileron and rudder trim on the EICAS STATUS and F/CTL page?

With the aircraft on the ground the neutral indication will be green. In the air the indication will be white regardless of trim position.

What is the purpose of the aileron disconnect function (roll disconnect)?

ROLL DISC allows the crew to separate the left control wheel and associated cable system from the right. This can be useful in case of a jammed aileron control system or a PCU runaway.

How are the left and right elevators connected?

During normal operations the left and right elevators are connected but can be separated in case of one being jammed. The two systems are separate except for the connection. The pilot controls the left elevator and the copilot controls the right.

What happens when the ROLL DISC handle is pulled?

This is used when an aileron jams. The control wheel interconnect (torque tube) is separated and it will advise the SSCUs that the interconnect torque tube has been disconnected. The pilot has control of the left aileron and the copilot has control of the right aileron.

Twenty seconds after pulling the ROLL DISC handle, the SSCU will illuminate the two amber ROLL SEL lights on the glare shield to illuminate and display the EICAS caution SPOILERONS ROLL message. The pilots then need to determine which side is not jammed and select the ROLL SEL switchlight on the non-jammed side and this will provide the flying pilot with flight spoiler control.

Selecting the ROLL SEL will remove the amber ROLL SEL lights on the glare shield and the EICAS caution. The green PLT ROLL CMD or CPLT ROLL CMD will appear on glare shield and on the EICAS depending which ROL SEL switchlight was selected.

What does an amber ROLL SEL switchlight indicate?

The roll disconnect handle has been pulled.

What does a white spoiler on the flight control page indicate?

The spoiler has had a loss of redundancy.

What does an amber spoiler on the flight control page indicate?

The spoiler is inoperative.

What two situations would require the use of the ROLL DISC handle?

- A jammed aileron.
- An uncommanded displacement of an aileron PCU.

How many PCUs power the rudder?

3

How is rudder jam protection provided?

Anti-jam/breakout protection (spring tension breakout) is provided to both sets of pedals. In case of a jammed rudder control, both sets of pedals will remain working but additional pedal force will be required to move the rudder.

What happens when the RUD TRIM switch is turned left or right?

This switch moves the rudder control cables to move the rudder surface. NL and NR stands for nose left and nose right.

Will actuating the rudder trim cause the rudder peddles to move?

Due to the position of the rudder trim actuator, the trim will not cause the pedals to move.

Do all three rudder PCUs need to be operative for the rudder trim to move the rudder surface?

Only one PCU needs to be operative to actuate the rudder trim.

What is the purpose of the yaw dampers (YD)?

They improve directional stability and turn coordination. If these oscillations were not corrected by the YDs it could cause dutch roll.

Are the yaw dampers connected to the autopilot?

The yaw dampers operate separately.

What commands the movement of the yaw dampers?

The flight control computers (FCC) operate the yaw dampers. FCC 1 controls yaw damper 1 and FCC 2 control yaw damper 2.

What is the function of the YD 1 and YD 2 button on the YAW DAMPER panel?

They engage the associated yaw damper.

How are the yaw dampers disengaged?

- Disengagement is by the yaw damper DISC button on the YAW DAMPER panel.
- If the YD channel fails.
- Upon landing.

What occurs if both YDs fail?

If the autopilot is engaged it will disconnect and their will be an EICAS caution message that both YDs are off line.

What serves as a gust lock for the ailerons on the ground?

The flutter damper along with the PCUs serves as a gust lock. Hydraulic pressure is locked in the system to prevent movement.

Is there any gust lock protection for the rudder, ailerons or elevators?

When the hydraulic systems are depressurized, the trapped fluid will prevent movement.

How is pitch control provided?

By the elevators and assisted by a moveable horizontal stabilizer.

How many PCUs are provided for each elevator?

Three PCUs are on each elevator.

Explain the flutter dampers on the elevators.

No flutter dampers are installed on the elevators.

What happens when the PITCH DISC handle is pulled and turned?

The interconnection between the two elevators is removed. The operable control surface will be controlled by the pilot or co-pilot controls. If both surfaces are operable, the captain will control the left elevator and the FO will control the right elevator.

When the PITCH DISC handle is pulled and turned will there be an EICAS message?

No

When would the PITCH DISC be used?

The PITCH DISC would be used when an elevator is jammed.

What happens if there is a jammed elevator PCU?

It will be overpowered by the other two PCUs on that elevator.

What provides horizontal pitch trim?

The trim switches on the control yoke vary the horizontal stabilizer angle of incidence

How does the horizontal stabilizer mechanically move?

Two electric motors drive a jack screw to move the horizontal stabilizer.

What happens when STAB TRIM CH 1 and CH 2 switches are pressed?

Pressing these switches engages channel 1 and 2 of the horizontal stabilizer trim control unit (HSTCU). They are engage only switches.

What happens if a HSTCU motor has a runaway?

To prevent this each trim motor has a brake that automatically engages.

Where does the HSTCU receive inputs?

- Autopilot (AFCS)
- Mach trim system
- Control wheel trim switches

How is the STAB TRIM disengaged?

The pilots can disconnect the stabilizer trim by the pitch/trim disconnect button on either control wheel. The horizontal stabilizer is monitored and if there is a fault, the stab trim will be disengaged automatically. This will be indicated on the EICAS by a white status message STAB CH 1 OR 2 INOP if one channel fails and an amber caution message STAB TRIM if both channels fail.

What is happening if you hear a clacker sound?

This could be a possible runaway trim. If the stabilizer trim is in motion for more than 3 seconds the clacker will sound. This can also occur if a pilot activates the stabilizer trim for more than 3 seconds.

What is the purpose of the Mach trim?

As Mach speed increases above 0.4 the Mach trim will make allowances for the rearward shift of the aerodynamic center of pressure. A negative stick force gradient and a decrease in longitudinal stability (Mach tuck) will occur above Mach 0.4 while hand flying if this correction did not occur.

How do you engage the Mach trim?

Press the MACH TRIM switchlight. Both channels of the HSTCU must be powered and at least one STAB TRIM channel engaged.

What is the priority order for the stabilizer trim?

1. Manual trim
2. Autopilot trim
3. AFCS auto trim function (flaps/slats between 0-30°)
4. Mach trim

What is auto trim?

When the flaps are moving between 0-30° up or down with no other inputs from the autopilot or the pilots, there is a change in the aerodynamic center of pressure because of the flap movement. The auto trim will compensate for these changes by trimming the horizontal stabilizer.

Explain the different rates at which the stab trim moves.

- Pilot manual trim moves the stabilizer at the highest rate of movement.

- Copilot manual trim moves the stabilizer at the highest rate of movement.

- Autopilot has two rates of stabilizer movement. There is a high rate of trim when the flaps are extending or retracting and a low rate when the flaps are not moving.

- Mach trim moves the stabilizer at the slowest rate.

What sends the signal for the need for Mach trim?

Both FCCs must demand trim before the HSTCU will adjust the stabilizer as a function of Mach number with the autopilot not engaged and hand flying the airplane.

What must be operating for the Mach trim to function?

Both channels of the HSTCU must be powered and at least one STAB TRIM channel engaged.

How is the Mach trim disengaged?

Pressing the MACH TRIM switchlight after it has been engaged or press the stab trim disconnect on either control wheel.

What are the primary flight controls?

- Ailerons
- Elevators
- Rudder
- Multifunction flight spoilers (since the MFS assist with roll control they are part of the primary and secondary flight controls)

What are the secondary flight controls?

- Outboard and inboard flaps
- Rudder trim, aileron trim and horizontal stab trim
- Slats
- Multifunction spoilers
- Ground lift dumping devices
- Flaps

What is the stabilizer trim priority order?

1. Pilot manual trim
2. Co-pilot manual trim
3. Autopilot
4. Auto trim
5. Mach trim

What will alert the crew if the airspeed is too high for the selected flap setting?

If the airspeed is too high for the flap setting an overspeed aural warning will sound.

What EICAS message will appear if one channel of the FECU fails?

The message will be FLAP HALF SPEED.

What happens if one of the two power drive motors that move the slat/flaps fail?

The system will operate at half speed.

What is the design of the flaps?

The flaps are double slotted fowler flaps that move rearward and down.

Explain the mechanics of what happens when the flap lever is moved to the 8° position.

An electrical command is sent from the slat/flap electronic control unit (SFECU) to start flap movement. The flap brakes are released and the two AC power drive units (PDU) turn the flap gearbox, which rotates flex shafts to move the flap ball screw actuators. When 8 degrees is reached the PDUs are de-energized and the flap brakes are applied. This is the same process for any flap movement.

When will the flap position indicator appear on the EICAS primary page?

When at least one of the following occur:

- The flaps are greater than zero degrees.
- Brake temperature monitoring system (BTMS) is in the red range.
- The landing gear is not up and locked.

When will the flap indication be removed from the EICAS primary page?

When all of the following occur in flight:

- Gear is up and locked.
- BTMS is normal, not in red.
- The flaps are up.

When will the flaps operate at half speed?

If there is a failure of a single PDU or one SFECU channel. It will be indicated as a FLAP HALFSPEED status message.

What will happen if the SFECU detects a fault?

An amber EICAS FLAPS FAIL message will appear and the flaps will stop.

What EICAS page will always display flap position?

The EICAS F/CTL page will always display flap position.

What spoilers make up the ground lift dump system (GLD)?

The inboard and outboard MFS along with the inboard and outboard ground spoilers make up the GLD system. All spoiler panels make up the GLD system.

What is the purpose of the GLD system?

The system aids during touchdown and after a rejected takeoff to spoil lift and increase drag to help stop the aircraft.

Where do the SSCUs get information to operate the automatic and manual modes of the GLD system?

- Proximity sensor electronic unit (PSEU), weight on wheels function.

- Thrust lever position micro switches.

- Wheel speed from the anti-skid control unit.

- The radio altimeter.

How could the pilot manually retract the GLD after landing?

Selecting the SPOILERS switch to MAN DISARM to manually retract the GLD.

What conditions are necessary for the GLD to be armed for takeoff when the spoilers switch is in the AUTO position?

- Left or right engine thrust greater than MIN TAKEOFF.

- Wheel speed greater than 45 knots.

- WOW.

- Radio altitude.

What happens to the GLD system if a touch and go landing is necessary?

If the thrust levers are advanced the GLD will retract and the system will re-arm.

What conditions are necessary for the GLD system to deploy?

Thrust levers idle and two of the following three: RA<10 feet, wheel spin up, WOW. The spoilerons will not extend until both main wheels are WOW. This is to assist with roll control.

What controls the deploying, retracting and arming of the GLD?

SSCUs

Explain the AUTO position of the SPOILERS switch.

The GLD system is automatically armed when the aircraft is configured for takeoff or landing and certain conditions are met.

Explain the MAN ARM position of the SPOILERS switch.

If the AUTO function fails the GLD system can be manually armed.

Explain the MAN DISARM position of the SPOILERS switch.

During malfunctions with the automatic arming or disarming of the GLD, the system can be manually disarmed with this switch.

What monitors the aircraft systems for correct configuration and operation?

The proximity sensing system (PSS). The PSS consists of the proximity sensing electronic unit (PSEU), which receives information from the proximity switches, proximity sensors and micro switches. The PSEU then sends the information to command the operation of other aircraft subsystems. The subsystems are the stall warning system, HSTCU, SFECU, SSCU.

What helps the crew in directional control with a jammed rudder?

The anti-jam/breakout system of the rudder. It will take a little more rudder pressure from the pilot or copilot, but the pilots will be able to override the jammed rudder.

What controls spoiler operation?

The operation of the spoilers is controlled by two dual channel spoiler and stabilizer control units (SSCUs).

What is the job of the flight spoilers?

They provide speed control and lift dumping.

What are the types of spoiler panels located on the top of each wing?

The panels are the inboard and outboard multifunction spoilers and outboard and inboard ground spoiler for a total of four on each wing.

What are the extended positions of the flight spoilers?

Any position between 0 to the maximum of 50° is the extended position.

What does an amber X on a spoiler outline indicate?

The input data is invalid.

How can a takeoff configuration warning be canceled?

Cancellation only occurs by retarding the thrust levers or correcting the configuration problem that created the warning.

What is the purpose of the stall protection system (SPS)?

If there is an impending stall this system provides aural, visual, and tactile warnings. It will also try to prevent the stall with a stick pusher.

What does the SPS monitor?

- Left and right angle of attack (AOA) vanes.

- Lateral acceleration through the AHRS system.

- Slat and flap position (SFECU).

- Weight on wheels.

- Mach speed - Mach transducers and ADCs 1 and 2.

What does the SPS do when a high angle of attack (AOA) is approached?

First the continuous (CONT) ignition is activated and if the AOA continues to increase, the stick shaker is activated followed by the autopilot disengaging. If after all of this the AOA is still increased, the stick pusher is activated, the STALL switchlights on the glare shield flash and the warbler sounds.

What happens to the SPS system if the AOA is increased rapidly?

If the AOA is increased at a rate greater than 1° per second, the SPS will lower the point of stall warning activation. The SPS will give the stall warnings at a lower AOA.

Once the stick pusher is activated, what will disconnect it?

- If less than 0.5G is sensed by an acceleration switch.

- Press and hold either the pilot or copilot autopilot/stick pusher disconnect switch (AP/SP DISC).

- Select one or both STALL PTCT PUSHER switch to OFF.

Does the AP/SP DISC button need to just be pressed and released to disengage the stick pusher?

It must be pressed and held to disengage the stick pusher as long as the activation is enabled. Otherwise if the AP/SP DISC button is release and the pusher conditions are met the SPS system will reengage the stick pusher.

If only one STALL PTCT PUSHER switch is selected ON, will the stick pusher engage if the activation point was met?

Both of the STALL PTCT PUSHER switches must be selected ON.

What message will appear if the AP/SP DISC switch was pressed and held for more than 4 seconds?

A STALL FAIL caution message will appear on the EICAS. When the switch is release the message will disappear.

How is the SPS system tested?

The test is accomplished on the ground by pressing either STALL switchlight on the glare shield. Any fault will be sent to the DCU for aural and/or visual annunciation.

How will the pilot know if an aileron flutter damper failed or had low fluid?

Looking at the EICAS flight control page the aileron flutter damper will be white and a status message of FLUTTER DAMPER displayed.

What does an amber boxed E on the PFDs indicate?

With the autopilot engaged this indicates a horizontal stabilizer mistrim.

What does an amber boxed A on the PFDs indicate?

With the autopilot engaged this indicates an aileron mistrim condition.

What does an amber boxed R on the PFDs indicate?

With the autopilot engaged this indicates a rudder mistrim condition.

How are the aileron, elevator and rudder surfaces moved?

Through the controls on the flight deck, control movement is transmitted via cable and/or push rods to the power control units (PCU) that hydraulically move the surface.

How many PCUs are on each aileron?

2

What does the takeoff configuration warning system monitor?

The position of the following:

- Slat/flaps
- Spoilers
- Autopilot
- Parking brake
- Aileron trim
- Rudder trim
- Horizontal stabilizer trims

When is the takeoff configuration warning system armed?

When the aircraft is on the ground the configuration system is armed.

What indicates the aircraft is in takeoff configuration?

The green T/O CONFIG O/K advisory message on the EICAS status page indicates the aircraft is configured for takeoff. This message is removed at aircraft rotation or anytime T/O configuration is not met.

What happens if the takeoff configuration warning system senses an unsafe takeoff configuration?

When both engines are above 70% N1, the master warning will flash, aural alerts sound and warning messages are presented on the EICAS. Which EICAS and aural warnings occur depends on what caused the alert.

chapter 9

Flight Instruments

How many air data computers are installed?

Three air data computers are installed; two are primary and one for the ISI.

What powers the integrated standby instrument (ISI)?

The ISI is DC powered by the battery bus.

Where does the ISI receive localizer and glide slope information?

The ISI receives LOC and GS information from RTU 1 or the standby tuning unit when turned on.

What formats can be selected on the multi-function display (MFD)?

- Radar
- FMS plan map
- TCAS
- FMS map
- Navaid sector
- HSI

What is the purpose of the display reversionary panel (DRP)?

The switch is used to change the format on the associated MFD to a PFD or EICAS format.

What is the purpose of the source selector panel?

If there is a failure of an air data computer, attitude/heading computer, EICAS or display control panel (DCP), this panel will allow an alternate source for the system to be selected. This panel controls the data source for the EFIS system.

Explain the ATT HDG switch on the source selector panel.

- NORM: The pilot and co-pilot electronic flight displays receive data from onside AHRS.

- Position 1 and 2: The pilot and copilot electronic flight displays receive data from AHRS 1 in position 1 and AHRS 2 in position 2. There will be an amber message on the PFD and or MFD displaying the source.

Explain the AIR DATA switch on the source selector panel.

- NORM: The pilot and co-pilot electronic flight displays receive data from the on-side air data computer (ADC).

- Position 1 and 2: The pilot and copilot electronic flight displays will display data from ADC 1 in position 1 and ADC 2 in position 2. On both PFDs there will be displayed an amber ADC 1 or 2 depending on selection.

Explain the DSPL CONT switch on the source selector panel.

- NORM: The pilot and copilot electronic flight displays are controlled by the respective DCPs.

- Position 1 and 2: In position 1, the pilot and copilot electronic flight displays are controlled by the pilot's DCP. In position 2, the copilot DCP controls the pilot and copilot electronic flight displays. On both MFDs and PFDs there will be an amber source message.

Explain the EICAS switch on the source selector panel.

When either ED1 or ED2 EICAS display fails, the remaining operative ED can display all EICAS pages.

Example: ED1 fails and the primary page automatically transfers to ED2 and this makes the ECP inactive. To regain the use of the ECP, select ED2 on the source selector panel. This will reactivate the ECP and all pages can now be displayed on ED2. If ED2 fails, selecting ED1 allows all pages to be viewed on ED1 through the ECP.

What is the name of the panel that allows airspeeds to be set?

The air data reference panel (ARP).

What is the name of the panel that allows the NAV SOURCE to be set?

The display control panel (DCP).

What is the name of the panel that allows autopilot commands to be set?

The flight control panel (FCP).

Explain the EFIS comparison monitor.

The primary flight display (PFD) continuously monitors itself in comparison to the other PFD. When the EFIS PFDs detect a comparison disagreement between each other an amber EFIS COMP MON is displayed on the primary page of the EICAS. The data message associated with the disagreement will flash for 5 seconds on the PFDs and then stay steady as long as the comparison error exists.

What does an amber HDG message on the PFDs indicate?

There is a difference of more than 6 degrees between each AHRS.

What does an amber ROL message on the PFDs indicate?

There is a difference between AHRS of more than 4 degrees roll or 3 degrees if the glide slope is captured.

What does the amber PIT message on the PFDs indicate?

There is a difference between AHRS of more than 4 degrees pitch or 3 degrees after the glide slope is captured.

What does the amber IAS message on the PFDs indicate?

There is a difference of more than 10 knots between PFDs.

What does the amber ALT message on the PFDs indicate?

There is more than 60 feet difference between PFDs.

What does the amber LOC message on the PFDs indicate?

There is a difference between the localizer receivers.

What does the amber GS message on the PFDs indicate?

There is a difference between the glide slope receivers.

What does the amber RA message on the PFDs indicate?

There is a difference between the radio altimeters below 1000 feet AGL.

What systems do the pitot static system supply information to?

- Air data computers (ADC)
- Stall protection system (SPS)
- Cabin pressure acquisition module (CPAM)
- Standby air data system (ADS)

Where is the total air temperature (TAT) probe located?

The TAT probe is located under the copilot's side window.

Explain the TAT probe.

Total air temperature is determined by this probe and supplied to all ADCs. The ADCs then use the TAT information to calculate and display on the EFIS the true airspeed (TAS), static air temperature (SAT), and total air temperature (TAT).

How is the DH/MDA removed from the PFD?

When displayed, it can be removed by pressing the center of the DH/MDA knob.

How can individual speeds be removed from the PFD?

When the speed is selected, pressing the center of the SPEED REFS knob will remove the speed displayed at that time.

What would indicate a good test of the radio altimeter?

Press the RA TEST button and the RA should indicate 50 feet. When the button is release, the reading should return to 0.

How is the speed reference manually changed between Mach and IAS?

Press the center of the SPEED KNOB.

Explain the low and high-speed cues.

The checkerboard at the top and bottom of the airspeed scale indicates these cues. The top indicates Vmo/Mmo and the bottom indicates a calculated airspeed of 1.06Vs.

Explain the airspeed trend vector.

The trend vector moves in response to the aircraft acceleration or deceleration. It indicates the predicted speed in 10 seconds.

When will the Mach window appear in the top left corner of the PFD?

The Mach window will appear when the aircraft speed is above Mach .45 and removed when the speed is below .40 Mach.

What is the range of the of the barometric altitude readout?

-1,000 to 50,000 feet

What happens to the altitude alert when the aircraft is passing through 1,000 feet above or below the pre-selected altitude?

There is an aural tone and the pre selected altitude bugs flash.

What happens when the aircraft deviates from the selected altitude?

When the deviation reaches 200 feet from the pre-selected altitude, an aural tone is heard and the pre-selected altitude indicators flash yellow. When the altitude deviation is minor the pre-selected altitude flashes magenta.

What is meant when the pre-selected altitude turns cyan?

The altitude tracking between the ADCs is outside tolerances.

What is the range of the MDA setting?

The range of the MDA setting is 0 to 15,000 feet.

What is the range of the vertical speed field?

The scale range is 0 to +/- 4,000 fpm. The digital readout ranges from 0 to 15,000 feet.

What else can be displayed on the VSI other than vertical speed?

TCAS advisory deviations.

What is the range of the radio altitude display?

-20 to 2,500 feet AGL

What are the different colors of the radio altitude display?

The digital readout is green from decision height (DH) to 2,500 feet and amber equal or lower than DH.

What happens if the radio altitude fails?

An RA in a red box appears and the RA tape and digit readouts are removed.

Where is altitude information presented other than the normal radio altimeter digital readout provided?

Next to the altitude tape is a scale, which indicates altitudes from 0 to 1,100 feet. The indication is green but turns amber at DH and then turns green again at touchdown.

What is the digital range selection of the decision height display?

0 to 999

What will happen if the ADC airspeed, vertical speed or altitude fails?

Red air data flags will replace the system information on the PFD.

What warning is provided if the aircraft descends to a negative altitude?

A yellow NEG is displayed next to the altimeter on the PFD

What system supplies the attitude and heading information?

Attitude and heading reference system (AHRS)

What components does the AHRS system consist of?

The AHRS system is made up of 2 computers, 2 flux detector units and 2 remote compensator units.

What panel provides AHRS mode selections?

The COMPASS control panel.

When is the DG mode on the compass control panel used?

DG mode is used when the aircraft is in an area of magnetic field disruptions or failure of heading information from the AHRS system. It is not intended for long term use.

How long does it take the AHRS to initialize?

Initialization occurs automatically when electrical power is established with the aircraft stationary. In MAG mode initialization takes approximately 70 seconds and 10 minutes in DG mode.

What provides rate and acceleration data for the AHRS computer?

Two sensors for each AHRS computer provide rate and acceleration. These sensors have four pairs of piezoelectric accelerometer sensors that are on a rotating wheel.

Explain the SLEW switch on the COMPASS control panel.

The switch is operational in DG and MAG mode. In MAG mode it will cause the displayed heading to move but it will move back to its original position when the slew switch is released. In DG mode the SLEW switch will cause the heading to slew in the direction selected and it will remain in position when released.

What happens when DG is selected on the COMPASS control panel?

The flux detector data no longer provides heading information.

Can the aircraft be moved during the AHRS ground alignment process?

The aircraft should not be moved. The PFD will display the message ATT/HDG ALIGNING DO NOT TAXI during the alignment process. If there is motion detected during the alignment process, the AHRS will re-initialize.

Can the AHRS conduct the alignment process in flight?

Airborne alignment is possible and will take 10 to 35 seconds. This would be needed if there were a power interruption. Most of the same flags on the PFD that appear during the ground alignment will appear in flight. The aircraft should remain in straight and level flight.

What buses provide power to AHRS 1 and AHRS 2?

AHRS 1 is powered by the DC ESS BUS and AHRS 2 is powered by DC BUS 2. If power to the bus is lost the affected AHRS will be powered by the battery bus. On battery power the AHRS will power the AHRS for up to 11 minutes. The AHRS will not reinitialize or restart on the battery bus only.

What is the color of the glide slope triangle when showing onside and cross-side data?

The triangle is green for on-side and amber for cross-side.

What is the value of the two dots above and below the reference line for vertical deviation?

Each dot is 1/4 degree.

When the vertical deviation on the glide slope display senses excessive vertical deviation the triangle flashes in an amber color. How can this flashing amber be corrected?

The flashing amber diamond can only be canceled when the condition is corrected.

What happens if the glide slope information is not valid?

There will be a red-boxed GS flag in the position of the glide slope pointer and scale.

What is the purpose of the amber alpha margin indicator (AMI) during a wind shear indication?

The AMI represents the maximum pitch attitude allowed. This pitch attitude will be the pitch just before the activation of the stick shaker.

How long is the AMI displayed during a wind shear warning?

It is displayed a minimum of sixty seconds or until the aircraft has exited the wind shear condition.

What are the two types of wind shear conditions and how are they displayed?

The two types are increasing (caution) and decreasing performance (warning) wind shear. Increasing performance is indicated by an amber wind shear presented on the PFD with the AMI and FD.

During a decreasing performance wind shear, a red WINDSHEAR warning is presented on the PFD along with an aural "winds shear". The FD and the AMI is displayed.

What is the green line that moves around on the airspeed scale?

This is the low speed awareness Cue, which indicates 1.3Vs.

Explain the de-clutter function of the PFD.

During an unusual attitude all nonessential information is cleared from the PFD. The trip points for the de-clutter function are pitch angle in excess of +30 or -20 degrees, or roll in excess of 65 degrees. The only information presented is:

- Altitude
- Airspeed
- Attitude
- Vertical speed
- Compass
- Autopilot engage indicator

What occurs when the heading bug is selected off scale?

A dashed line appears from the center of the heading indicator to the bug and a digital heading indication will appear on the PFD.

What occurs when the heading or attitude information is invalid?

For heading information a red-boxed MAG, DG or TRUE will appear and the heading display is removed from the PFD. For attitude a red-boxed ATT appears and the attitude information is removed from the PFD.

If DME hold is on, will the FMS auto tune on that side?

No

How would you know if DME hold is activated?

An amber H replaces the NM of the navigation source indication on the PFD and the station identifier is removed. There is an amber H on the RTU next to the frequency.

Why is the station identifier removed from the navigation source indication when DME hold is activated?

The data for the identifier is supplied by the DME.

How would you find all the VOR and DME stations in use by the FMS?

Bring up the VOR/DME STATUS page and this will list all of the stations in use.

How are the bearing indications displayed on the PFD?

The BRG switches on the DCP.

What bearing indications can be presented on the PFD?

- VOR 1, VOR 2
- ADF 1, ADF 2
- FMS 1, FMS 2 (FMS 2 only on dual FMS aircraft)

What does the lateral deviation of the HSI needle equate to?

- Each dot equals 5 degrees in VOR.

- Each dot equals 1 degree in LOC.

- Each dot equals 5 NM in FMS.

What does an amber YD displayed on the upper left side of the attitude indicator indicate?

It indicates that both yaw dampers are disengaged.

What does an amber boxed A or E on the attitude indicator indicate?

An amber boxed A indicates that the FCC has detected an aileron out of trim condition. An amber boxed E indicates the FCC has detected an elevator out of trim condition.

How is a display control panel (DCP) failure indicated?

A red-boxed DCP flag on the PFD and MFD indicates failure of a DCP.

What occurs if a display has an over temperature?

When an over temperature condition is sensed, a red DISPLAY TEMP message will appear on the display. At this point all information is removed from the display but will return when the display cools.

What is the source of time data for the UTC clock on the top of the MFD?

The time is provided by the pilot's clock and if that fails, it will be provided by the copilot's clock.

How is weather radar displayed on the MFD?

Turn the radar on and select the WX/TERR button on the DCP.

What is the purpose of the NAV SOURCE selector switch on the DCP?

This selector is used to select the NAV source to be displayed on the MFD. The selections available are:

- HSI

- NAV SECTOR
- FMS MAP
- FMS PLAN MAP
- RADAR

What is the purpose of the PUSH X-SIDE button on the DCP NAV SOURCE selector knob?

The button allows for the selection of cross-side course information to be displayed when using the HSI and NAV sector formats.

Explain the purpose of the FMS plan map selection on the NAV SOURCE.

This map is used during flight plan set up and en route modifications. North will always be displayed at the top. The FMS legs page and FMS map can be used to verify the flight plan route by using the up or down keys on the FMS.

What MFD formats is the radar displayed on?

- Navaid sector map
- TCAS
- FMS map

What static system supplies the standby instruments?

The standby pitot static system (P3 and S3) supplies the standby instruments.

Where are the standby pitot tube and the standby static ports located?

The standby pitot tube is located on the left forward fuselage. A standby static port is located on each side of the forward fuselage.

What does the standby pitot static system provide data to?

- Integrated standby instrument (ISI)
- ISI ADC
- Cabin pressure acquisition module (CPAM)

What is the navigation source for the ISI localizer and glideslope?

The source is VHF navigation receiver 1 or the backup tuning unit. During normal operations the backup tuning unit will be in STBY and it will display what is selected in NAV and COM 1.

When would the CAGE button on the ISI be used?

The CAGE button will reset the horizon line during stabilized level flight. This button is not usable during power up.

What do +/- on the ISI control?

The buttons control the brightness.

What do the ADCs compute?

- Vertical speed.
- Indicated and pressure altitudes.
- True, indicated and calibrated airspeeds.
- Airspeed trend.
- Vertical speed and indicated airspeed references used by the flight director and auto flight systems.
- Mach number.
- Altitude alerting.
- Indications for Vmo/Mmo.
- Overspeed alerts for Vmo/Mmo.
- Temperature deviations from ISA.

What equipment provides the ADC with information?

- AHRS
- IAPS
- FDR
- Flap control unit and stall protection computer (ADC 1)
- FCC and FD
- Transponders and TCAS
- EFIS and EICAS

What bus powers AHRS 1 and 2?

AHRS 1 is powered by the DC essential bus and AHRS 2 is powered by DC BUS 2.

What will happen to the AHRS if the bus powering it lost power?

The AHRS powered by that bus would continue to operate for 11 minutes.

Will an AHRS re-initialize or restart on battery power only?

No

What component generates all indications on the MFDs and PFDs?

The integrated avionics processor system (IAPS).

What bus powers the PFDs and MFDs?

The DC ESS BUS powers the pilot PFD and MFD. DC BUS 2 powers the copilot PFD and MFD.

What equipment failed if the airspeed, altitude and VS information failed?

Onside ADC failed. The off-side ADC can be selected as a backup by using the AIR DATA knob on the source selector panel.

What has failed if the altitude and/or heading information on the PFD failed?

The AHRS on that side has failed. The off-side AHRS can be selected by using the ATTD HDG knob on the source selector panel.

What panel will be used if a display control panel (DCP) failed?

The DSPL CONT knob on the source selector panel. This allows a single DCP to provide data to both EFIS systems. Both PFDs will have an amber DCP 1 or 2 message.

What supplies the aircraft time information?

Standard style: The two clocks on the flight deck with the captain's clock as primary.

GPS style: Upon power up if there is a valid GPS signal the clocks will be automatically set. If there is not a GPS signal or there is a need manually override the GPS signal, then the pilots can set the clock.

What bus powers the GPS style pilot clock?

DC battery bus

What bus powers the GPS style copilot clock?

DC BUS 2 powers the GPS clock.

What bus powers both GPS style clocks?

Main battery direct bus

How can the GPS style clocks be set manually?

The pilot can select the time setting mode. The clocks will then not use GPS signals until the next time power is reset.

Explain how to set the GPS clock.

1. Press and hold the MODE button for 2 seconds.

2. Use the MODE button to toggle between UTC hours and minutes when the INT is displayed.

3. Continue to use the MODE button to set year, month and day when DT is displayed.

4. Continue to use the MODE button to set the local time hours and minutes when LT is displayed.

5. In any of the above modes the ET SEL is used to decrease the data and the ET RST is used to increase the data.

6. To exit the setting process, at any time press the MODE button for 2 seconds.

What is the ET and CHR button on the GPS clock?

ET is used for elapsed time and CHR is used for chronometer time.

What are the different modes of the MODE button on the GPS clock?

- DT
- GPS
- INT
- LT

How is the CHR started on the GPS style clock?

The first press will start the CHR, second will stop it and third press will reset by blanking the display.

How is the ET used on the GPS style clock to get elapsed time for the flight?

Select the ET SEL button before takeoff and this will display the ET annunciator. When the aircraft is airborne the digits will appear. At touchdown the counter will stop. To reset press the ET RST and the display will be blanked.

Can the ET RST on the GPS style clock be used in flight?

The ET RST is available only on the ground.

What bus powers the standard clocks if there is a power failure?

The main battery direct bus powers the standard clocks during a power failure.

Can the ET with a standard clock be reset in flight?

ET reset can only be used on the ground.

How is the standard clock set?

Select the SET position and use the CHR to change the value. ET will cycle through the modes.

chapter 10

Fuel

Can the center tank be gravity refueled?

No, only the wing tanks can be gravity refueled.

What is the total fuel capacity?

Pressurized refueling is 19,594 lb. and gravity refueling is 14,580 lb.

What must the bulk fuel temperature be above to depart?

-30°C or warmer

Where is the bulk fuel temperature measured?

The right wing tank is where the bulk fuel temperature is measured.

What provides static and dynamic venting for the fuel tanks?

NACA vent scoops under the wings provide static and dynamic venting.

What are the two methods of fueling?

The two methods are pressure and gravity fueling

Where are the collector tanks located?

The two collector tanks are located in the center tank at a point that is lower than the left or right wing tanks.

What provides fuel tank ventilation when the airplane is in a nose up attitude?

Ventilation is provided by a climb vent.

Explain the construction of the wing fuel tanks?

The wing tanks are a wet wing design. A sealant is used to seal the tanks so this makes the wing the tank.

Explain the fuel vent system.

The NACA scoops have vent lines connected to the tanks to provide static and dynamic pressure. In flight the NACA vents will provide ram air pressure to maintain a positive pressure on the fuel in the tanks.

Static ventilation of the tanks during ground operations is provided through the NACA vents. They will also relieve pressure caused by fueling or thermal expansion. To prevent fuel from coming out of the NACA vent when the aircraft is being refueled, the NACA vent line drains the fuel trapped in the vent lines back into the center tank.

During climb you notice the total fuel in the center tank increase by 300 lbs, is this a problem?

This is not a problem. It is possible for fuel to flow to the center tank from the vent system during climb and cause the fuel quantity readings of the center tank to increase as high as 300 lbs.

What monitors and controls the operation of the fuel system?

A dual-channel fuel system computer monitors and controls the operation of the fuel system.

Do both fuel computer channels operate at the same time?

One channel operates at a time. When the active channel fails, the standby channel will assume control.

Where is the temperature of the fuel measured?

- Right wing tank
- In the fuel line to each engine

Explain the general operation of ejector pumps.

Motive fuel flow must come from a source like the engine high-pressure fuel pump. This motive flow is passed through a Venturi shaped nozzle and the fuel exits the nozzle at an increased velocity that creates a low pressure. This low pressure creates a suction that draws fuel out of the tank.

What powers the fuel ejectors?

Motive flow from the engine high-pressure pump powers the fuel ejectors. High-pressure fuel flows through a Venturi shaped nozzle of the ejector, which creates a low pressure. This then draws fuel out of the tank by suction.

Explain how to manually measure the amount of fuel in the tanks?

Magnetic level indicators (MLI) are used to manually check the fuel amount in each tank. There is one MLI for the center tank and two for each wing tank.

To check the fuel level, release the measuring stick and let it drop. As the float magnet and the magnet on the stick come in line, the stick will stop. The uncorrected tank quantity is indicated on the stick. This indication is then corrected by referring to the two inclinometers mounted on circuit breaker panel 2 to determine aircraft roll and pitch deviation from level. Refer to the FCOM to find the quantity.

What information does the fuel computer gather to calculate the fuel weight in each tank?

The fuel computer gets information from the fuel system and aircraft attitude information from the AHRS to calculate fuel weight.

At what fuel imbalance will the fuel computer initiate fuel crossflow in automatic mode?

In automatic mode the correction will begin with an imbalance of 200 pounds between the main tanks.

What are the two methods to crossflow fuel?

- Powered crossflow (automatic or manual)

- Gravity crossflow

During automatic fuel crossflow when will the fuel transfer terminate?

The transfer will terminate when the wing tank that is receiving fuel is 50 lbs more than the other wing tank.

Which fuel tank transfers the fuel when the right wing tank is the low tank?

Fuel is actually drawn from both tanks by the bi-directional XFLOW pump. The crossflow valve on the low wing is opened to allow fuel to transfer to that wing.

Explain the manual powered crossflow operation.

This feature is used when the automatic powered crossflow does not respond to an imbalance. The pilot can select the XFLOW AUTO OVERRIDE switchlight to MANUAL, which will inhibit the automatic powered crossflow system.

The L or R crossflow SOV switchlight can be selected on the low tank side. Selecting this switchlight will cause the crossflow pump to activate. The pilot must turn off the crossflow by deselecting the L or R XFLOW AUTO OVERRIDE switchlight once balance is achieved.

What happens when the AUTO OVERRIDE switch is placed in MAN?

This inhibits the automatic crossflow system.

What happens when the L XFLOW or R XFLOW is selected after the AUTO OVERRIDE is activated?

This switch will activate the XFLOW pump and open the associated crossflow valve.

When will the FUEL IMBALANCE caution message appear on the EICAS?

When there is an imbalance of 800 lbs. (363 kg.) between the wing tanks.

Explain the gravity crossflow operation?

This operation is used when the power fuel crossflow does not correct the fuel imbalance or the XFLOW pump is inoperative. The pilot can manually select the GRAVITY XFLOW switchlight to open the gravity crossflow SOV. Fuel will flow through the gravity manifold to achieve a balance. The aircraft can be side slipped to help the fuel transfer.

What will happen if both L and R XFLOW switchlights are selected to manual crossflow mode?

The crossflow pump will not be powered and the XFLOW PUMP caution message will be annunciated. Both XFLOW FAIL switchlights will illuminate. Crossflow is inhibited until AUTO OVERRIDE switchlight is deselected or one of the XFLOW switchlights is deselected.

What happens when the GRAVITY/XFLOW switchlight is pressed?

The gravity XFLOW SOV is opened, a white OPEN illuminates on switchlight and EICAS displays a green GRAV XFLOW OPEN.

What does the amber FAIL light in the GRAVITY XFLOW switchlight indicate?

The gravity XFLOW SOV is not in the commanded position.

What is required of the pilots to transfer fuel from the center tank to the wing tanks?

This process is completely automatic. The transfer ejectors perform the transfer of fuel from the center tank to the wing tanks. This process does require motive flow, which means the engines need to be operating.

What EICAS messages are displayed when fuel is transferred from the center tank to the wing tanks?

There are no EICAS messages or indications.

Explain the process of transferring fuel from the center tank to the wing tanks.

This process is automatic and controlled by the fuel system computer. Transfer begins when the fuel level in a wing tank drops below 94% of its capacity and there is fuel in the center tank. The appropriate fuel transfer valve will open, motive flow from the engine feed manifold flows through the open valve to the transfer ejector, which will transfer fuel from the center tank to the appropriate wing tank.

When the respective wing tank is full, the transfer valve will close. When the wing is 94% full, with fuel in the center tank, the process starts over. This is the same process for both wing tanks.

Will fuel transfer from the center tank to the main tank during single engine taxi?

Fuel will still transfer from the center tank but only to the side with the engine operating. Motive flow is required for the transfer ejector to operate and that means an engine needs to be operating.

How is fuel transferred from the wing tanks to the collector tanks?

Fuel is transferred by scavenge ejectors. A scavenge ejector is located at the lowest inboard point of each wing tank.

How is fuel moved from the collector tank to the high pressure engine driven fuel pump?

There is one main ejector pump for each collector tank that provides fuel to the high pressure pump. Motive flow to operate the main ejector is provided by the high-pressure output of the engine driven fuel pump.

How are the boost pumps powered?

The boost pumps are DC powered.

What is the purpose of the electric boost pumps?

- Transfer fuel from the collector tanks to the engines.
- As a backup to the main ejectors when the ejector fails.
- Provide fuel pressure during engine start.

When will the electric boost pumps operate with the L and R boost pump switchlight selected?

Both pumps will operate when the fuel computer detects low fuel feed pressure in either feed manifold.

Where does the APU receive its fuel?

The fuel comes from the left collector tank by the APU pump.

Explain the transfer ejectors?

There are two transfer ejectors located in the aft section of the center tank and perform the job of transferring fuel from the center tank to the wing tanks. Motive flow created by the high-pressure output of the main ejectors operates the transfer ejectors.

Explain the engine fuel shutoff valves (SOV).

The associated ENGINE FIRE PUSH switchlight on the glare shield electrically controls the SOV. The purpose is to stop the flow of fuel to the engines. The ENGINE FIRE PUSH switchlight is located on the EMERGENCY BUS so it is always powered.

Where is the engine fuel temperature indication located?

Fuel temperature indication is on the FUEL synoptic page.

During normal engine operation what are the electric boost pumps doing?

With the boost pump switchlights activated the boost pumps are in standby mode. If a main ejector fails or does not supply enough pressure the boost pumps will activate automatically.

What are the two jobs of the boost pumps?

The boost pumps provide fuel pressure for engine starting and as backup to the main ejectors incase of failure.

How is the fuel heated before it enters the engine?

The fuel is heated by a fuel/oil heat exchanger located on each engine. Hot engine oil passes through the heat exchanger to heat the fuel.

How many fuel filters are installed?

One fuel filter per engine.

What will happen if a fuel filter becomes contaminated?

An impending bypass switch monitors the filter for contamination. If a low fuel pressure is sensed, an EICAS message will alert the crew and the filter is bypassed so fuel can still be provided to the engine.

Is it normal for one electric boost pump to operate?

Under normal conditions both boost pumps operate at the same time.

How is defueling accomplished?

The two methods of defueling are suction and gravity. After attaching the single point adapter, the fuel control panel can be configured to apply suction to extract fuel. Gravity defuel is accomplished by fuel drain valves on the lowest point of each tank.

Where are the refueling/defueling operations controlled?

On the right side of the aircraft located near the wing root is a refuel/defuel control panel.

Explain how to refuel in the auto mode.

Select the total fuel quantity desired through the Increase/Decrease switch and then select the refuel start switch to ON. The fuel computer will direct the fuel to the appropriate tanks and stop fueling when the select amount is reached.

Explain how to refuel in the manual mode.

Fuel is directed to a tank by selecting open or closed the appropriate shutoff valve.

How does the fuel computer stop fueling when the tank is full?

High-level sensors stop fueling by sending a signal to the fuel computer to close the appropriate tank refuel SOV.

What does the INOP light in the boost pump switchlights indicate?

The INOP light indicates the boost pump is not armed (switch is pressed out), pump failed or low pump pressure.

What does the FAIL light in the GRAVITY XFLOW switchlight indicate?

The gravity crossflow SOV is not in the commanded position.

What does the ON light in the L or R XFLOW switchlight indicate?

The ON light will illuminate when the respective crossflow pump activates.

What does the FAIL light in the L or R XFLOW switchlight indicate?

In either auto or manual mode the associated crossflow pump did not activate with the right or left crossflow pump switchlight selected.

What does an illuminated XFLOW AUTO OVERRIDE MAN switchlight indicate?

Automatic crossflow is disabled and the crossflow pump is ready for manual crossflow.

What is the purpose of the BITE INITIA button on the refuel/defuel control panel?

When the FAULT ANNUNC is illuminated pressing this button will display the fault codes.

What will happen after selecting the TEST position on the refuel/defuel control panel?

The following will occur:

- SOV CL lights extinguish.
- SOV OP lights illuminate.
- H LEVEL DETECTOR illuminates.
- SOV OP lights extinguish.
- SOV CL lights illuminate.

When will the EICAS fuel quantity indications be green?

The indications are green when each wing tank has at least 600 pounds and the total fuel is greater than 1200 pounds.

When will the EICAS fuel quantity indications display an amber color?

The indications will turn amber when there is a fuel imbalance or a tank has less than 600 lbs. The total fuel quantity will also turn amber if less than 1200 pounds.

At what quantity will the center tank fuel indication turn amber?

The center tank fuel quantity indication can only be green or white. Green indicates quantity is greater than 10 lbs and white is less than 10 lbs.

At what bulk fuel temperature will the BULK FUEL TEMP caution message appear?

-40°C

What switches control the APU fuel feed SOV?

The APU FIRE PUSH switchlight and the PWR FUEL switchlight control the APU fuel feed SOV.

What switchlight controls the engine fuel feed SOV?

The left or right ENG FIRE PUSH switchlight controls the respective fuel feed SOV.

What temperature must the fuel be for the fuel feed temperature to be green?

At least 5°C for the fuel feed temperature to be green.

Explain the APU fuel shutoff valve (SOV).

The APU SOV is used to stop the flow of fuel to the APU. This SOV is opened and closed by the APU FIRE PUSH switchlight or by the PWR FUEL switchlight on the APU control panel.

Why should you never remove the gravity filler caps if the wing tanks are full or fuel quantity is not know?

The caps are located below the maximum pressure refueling level and fuel could come out if opened.

Can either boost pump provide pressurized fuel for the opposite engine fuel feed manifold?

There is a common fuel manifold between the boost pumps that allows the opposite boost pump to provide pressurized fuel to the other engine.

chapter 11

Hydraulics

How are the thrust reversers powered?

The right reverser is powered by hydraulic system 2 and the left is powered by hydraulic system 1.

If hydraulic system 3 is lost, what hydraulic system is used to lower the nose gear?

Hydraulic system 2 is used to release the over center lock when the alternate gear extension is used.

What hydraulic system powers the nose doors?

No hydraulic power is used to operate the nose doors.

How many PCUs power the multi-function spoilers (MFS)?

Each is powered by a single PCU from a single hydraulic system. With this setup the other panel will still operate with a single hydraulic system failure.

On the hydraulic shutoff valve panel, what do the switchlights operate?

The switchlights close the respective hydraulic shutoff valve. When selected closed the switchlight will illuminate a white CLOSED. This switchlight will isolate an engine driven pump from the hydraulic system without having to shutdown the engine. This is the same SOV controlled by the engine fire switchlight.

When the right hydraulic SOV switchlight is selected, what pump will this isolate?

The right engine driven hydraulic pump will be isolated. The electric hydraulic pump can still pressurize the system.

After pressing a hydraulic SOV switchlight, can the valve be opened again?

Yes, reselect the switchlight to open the valve.

When only one engine driven generator is operating, will a hydraulic B pump be shed?

No

When a hydraulic valve fails to attain the commanded position, what color will it turn?

Amber

How many hydraulic systems does the CRJ700 have?

The CRJ700 has a total of three hydraulic systems, which are identified as system 1, 2 and 3.

Which hydraulic pumps are engine driven?

Hydraulic system pump 1A and 2A is engine driven.

What is the normal PSI of the hydraulic systems?

3000 PSI

What is the only difference between hydraulic system 1 and 2 other than what they operate?

The reservoir capacities are different; system 2 is larger due to powering more equipment.

When do system 1A and 2A main hydraulic pumps operate?

Any time the respective engine is operating.

Which hydraulic pumps are electrically driven?

All backup pumps (B pumps) and the system 3A pump are all alternating current motor pumps. These are 1B, 2B, 3A, and 3B.

What is the color of Skydrol hydraulic fluid?

It is a purplish color and should not be touched, as it is highly corrosive.

Is there any kind of fluid exchange between hydraulic system 1 and 2?

No

In general, what systems are powered by at least one hydraulic system?

- Primary and secondary flight controls
- Wheel brakes
- Landing gear
- Nose wheel steering
- Thrust reversers

Specifically what systems do hydraulic system 1 power?

- Rudder
- Elevators
- L aileron
- OB MFS on each wing
- OB ground spoilers on each wing
- L thrust reverser

Specifically what systems do hydraulic system 2 power?

- Rudder
- Elevators
- Main landing gear auxiliary actuators
- Right aileron
- Right thrust reverser
- Main landing gear auxiliary actuators
- Inboard MFS on each wing
- Outboard brakes

Specifically what systems do hydraulic system 3 power?

- Left and right aileron
- Rudder
- Elevators
- IB ground spoilers
- Landing gear
- Nose wheel steering
- Inboard brakes

Which hydraulic system has the largest demand?

Hydraulic system 3 has the largest demand.

What is the job of the hydraulic accumulator?

The accumulator is used to store hydraulic pressure to satisfy the instantaneous demands of aircraft systems. It also dampens pressure surges within the system. The accumulator is charged with dry nitrogen.

How are hydraulic systems 1 and 2 cooled?

Because pumps 1A and 2A are within the engine nacelles and generate a lot of heat, the fluid needs to be cooled. The fluid is cooled by a ram air heat exchanger that is located in the aft equipment bay.

The air used by the heat exchanger for cooling is drawn in through the ram air scoop. The air is exhausted out the exit point on each side of the aft part of the fuselage and has a wire screen over the exhaust area. While on the ground an electric fan draws the air through the ram air scoop.

What pump serves as a back up to the left engine driven pump?

Alternating current motor pump (ACMP) 1B serves as a backup to the left engine driven pump.

How is the hydraulic SOVs closed?

The valves are shutoff by pressing the ENG FIRE PUSH switchlights or the HYD SOV switchlights on the HYDRAULIC panel.

Why does hydraulic system 3A and 3B not need a cooling system?

Hydraulic system 3A and 3B are not near a heat source so a dedicated cooling source is not needed.

What is the location of hydraulic system 3 main components and what are they?

The components are located in or near the main landing gear bay. The components are an accumulator, a reservoir and two AC pumps (3A, 3B).

When does the 3A pump operate?

During normal operations it runs continuously and is powered by an ON/OFF switch.

How is the hydraulic SOV for system 3 operated?

There is no hydraulic SOV like the SOVs for system 1 and 2.

What is the location of the ground service panels for the hydraulic systems?

For hydraulic systems 1 and 2 the service panel is in the aft equipment bay. The service panel for system 3 is located aft of the wing root on the right side of the fuselage.

Explain the ON switch position of hydraulic system 1 and 2.

This is the manual mode to operate hydraulic system 1 and 2 pumps. It will turn on pumps 1B and 2B.

What three things determine when the backup B pumps for system 1 and 2 will operate?

- Generator output
- Flap position
- Hydraulic switch position

Explain the AUTO switch position of hydraulic system 1 and 2.

Hydraulic pumps 1B and 2B will operate when they are powered, the flaps are not at zero, and associated generator is operating.

If you select the 1B or 2B hydraulic switch to ON with the aircraft on the ground and the engines not operating, will the pumps operate?

Yes, a circuit will allow the pumps to operate on the ground with the engine-driven generators not operating.

If pump 3A fails will 3B automatically take over?

Not automatically, but the pump can be manually turned on by selecting the 3B switch to ON.

When will the hydraulic pump 3B automatically energize?

When the ADG is deployed, pump 3B automatically energizes. When the 3B switch is in AUTO the pump will automatically operate when the flaps are extended and either generator is online.

Explain the AUTO position of the hydraulic pump 3B switch?

The pump will operate when the flaps are extended and either generator is online.

What will happen to the 3B pump if the switch is in the OFF position in flight and the ADG deploys due to loss of electrical power?

The 3B pump will operate because the emergency mode is independent of the 3B switch position.

While in flight with the hydraulic switches in AUTO and 3A in the ON position, what pumps are operating when the slats/flaps are extended?

All pumps will be operating during normal operations.

Will hydraulic 1B or 2B automatically start after an engine failure or hydraulic pump 1A or 2A failure?

No, the 1B or 2B hydraulic switch must be selected to ON under either of these condition.

While in cruise with the slats/flaps up, what pumps are operating?

1A, 3A, 2A

What is the purpose of the hydraulic SOV switchlights?

Without shutting down the respective engine the hydraulic engine driven pump can be isolated from the hydraulic system with these switchlights.

With the L HYD SOV pressed, can hydraulic system 1 still be pressurized by another source?

The 1B hydraulic pump in the ON position can pressurize hydraulic system 1.

When will the hydraulic system pressure indicate an amber caution range?

Less than 1800 PSI

On the hydraulic synoptic page, when will the reservoir quantity indicate green?

Green: >45% and <85%

What is the green range of the hydraulic system pressure?

1800 to 3200 PSI

When all hydraulic pressure is lost to the brakes, is there any braking capability?

There will be enough pressure for six brake applications due to the accumulators.

chapter 12

Ice and Rain Protection

When the ICE detector switchlight is pressed, what is being tested?

The three air data sensor heater controllers (ADSHC).

What happens when an ADSHC fails?

The probes associated with that ADSHC will switch to full heat.

Which areas of the aircraft are anti-iced?

- Wing leading edges
- Engine cowls
- Air data probes
- Windshields and flight side windows

How does the ice detector detect conditions that could lead to ice accumulation?

The ice detectors extend into the air stream and vibrate at high frequency. When ice accumulates on the probe the frequency of the vibration is dampened and the microprocessor sends a signal to the DCU to display an ICE caution message. The ICE DET switchlight on the ANTI-ICE control panel will also illuminate.

How will the ice detector know when the aircraft has exited ice conditions?

The ice detector electrically heats the probe for 5 seconds during each 60-second cycle. After heating the probe, if it does not accumulate any more ice, then the indication is removed.

What are the components of the ice detector system?

The system consists of two microprocessors and a probe on each side of the aircraft. These two systems are independent of each other. When the microprocessor detects ice on the probe, a signal is sent to the data concentrator units (DCU) and an amber caution ICE message is displayed.

After the ice detector detects ice and the wing and cowl anti-ice systems are turned on, how will the ice warning change?

It changes from an amber ICE message to an advisory green ICE message. The green ICE occurs when there is sufficient heat to the wings and the cowl anti-ice valves open.

Explain the ICE DET TEST switchlight on the ANTI-ICE panel.

When pressed for 5 seconds the ice detection system, air data probe heaters and the 3 ADSHCs are tested. A good test is indicated by illumination of the DET TEST switchlight and a caution ICE message on the EICAS if the temperature of the wing is below 18°C. If the temperature of the wing is above 18°C then a green advisory ICE message will be displayed. An ADS HEAT TEST OK advisory message will be displayed if the test passes.

During flight when will the DET ICE TEST switchlight illuminate?

Anytime the ice detector senses ice accumulation.

How is bleed air directed onto the wing leading edge?

Piccolo tubes direct hot bleed air onto the inner surface of the leading edges.

How does the bleed air exit after heating the wing leading edge?

The bleed air used to heat the fixed leading edge is vented through the wing leading edge structure and the forward fuselage fairing. The bleed air used to heat the slat exits between the upper fixed wing surface and the slat.

What is the normal position of the wing anti-ice cross-bleed valve?

Closed

What valves does the WING OFF-ON switch control?

The switch controls the left and right wing anti-ice valves.

What controls and monitors the wing anti-ice system?

Dual channel anti-ice leak detection controller (AILC) controls and monitors the wing anti-ice system.

Are both channels of the AILC controlling the wing anti-ice and leak detection systems at the same time?

Only one channel is in operation while the other is in standby.

Explain the temperature sensors in the wing.

There are two temperature sensors in each wing, an inboard and an outboard. Temperature is controlled by the inboard sensor sending information to the AILC so it can control the wing anti-ice valves. The outboard sensors monitor the temperature at the outboard end of the wings and checks for bleed air leaks.

What happens to the wing anti-ice temperature when the slats are extended?

A higher temperature will be maintained by the AILC.

What system controls a wing overheat condition?

The AILC controls a wing overheat condition.

What happens to the wing anti-ice system when the thrust reversers are activated?

Nothing

Can both wings be anti-iced when an engine fails?

Yes, the wing anti-ice cross bleed valve allows both wings to be anti-iced when an engine fails, engine bleed valve fails or an anti-ice valve fails.

Explain the NORMAL position of the WING A/I CROSS BLEED selector.

The wing cross-bleed valve is in the closed position.

Explain the FROM LEFT position of the WING A/I CROSS BLEED selector.

The right wing anti-ice valve is closed and the wing cross-bleed valve is open.

Explain the FROM RIGHT position of the WING A/I CROSS BLEED selector.

The left wing anti-ice valve is closed and the wing cross-bleed valve is open.

What is the meaning of an amber L or R WING A/ICE message?

The indicated wing has a low temperature condition or the anti-ice system has failed. The wing anti-ice switch must be on.

When the wing anti-ice is selected ON, what happens to the N2 gauge?

The N2 gauges show a variable white arc that indicates an advisory range for proper anti-icing of the wings. It is recommended to maintain a power setting above this white arc.

What happens when there is a wing overheat condition?

Sensors along the wing anti-icing dusk will send a signal to the DCUs and then display a WING OVHT warning on the EICAS primary page. There will also be an aural "wing overheat" warning. The A/ICE synoptic page will indicate the duct location of the overheat condition.

What position do the wing anti-ice valves fail to?

The valves are spring loaded closed.

What is required for the wing anti-ice valves to open?

When the wing anti-ice is selected to ON the valves will not open unless electrical power and bleed air is available.

What position do the engine anti-ice valves fail?

The engine anti-ice valves fail open.

Is a cowl anti-ice pressure relief valve installed?

The PRSOVs control pneumatic pressure to the cowls and protect from an overpressure condition.

Is the engine nose cone anti-iced?

The engine nose cone is anti-iced by engine oil.

What does a L or R COWL A/ICE DUCT warning message indicate?

If the inner wall of the engine cowl leading edge develops a leak, a bleed leak detector located on the outer wall will activate this message. Basically this is a duct within a duct.

What does a L or R COWL A/ICE DUCT status message indicate?

The cowl duct pressure is high or low.

What is opening when the LH or RH COWL ON/OFF switch is selected to ON?

The cowl anti-ice switch controls the respective cowl anti-ice SOV. These valves are pneumatically operated and electrically controlled.

What happens to the PRSOVs if the cowl anti-ice is on and the thrust reversers are deployed?

The PRSOVs close when the thrust reversers are deployed.

What does a L or R COWL A/ICE amber caution message indicate?

The associated cowl anti-ice valve is selected ON and the valve has failed to open or valve position is not known.

What is the purpose of the T2 probe in the engine?

This probe provides engine air inlet temperature to the FADEC.

How is the T2 probe anti-iced?

The probe is electrically heated and the heating is controlled by the FADEC.

Explain how the T2 probe is tested for proper operation?

The FADEC will test the T2 probe after engine shutdown on the ground. Electrical power must be maintained on the aircraft for at least one minute to allow the FADEC time to complete the test. The FADEC will test the T2 heater by energizing the heater and checking for the correct rise in temperature in 30 seconds.

Explain the L/R ENG TAT HEAT caution message.

During the T2 probe test after engine shutdown if the FADEC cannot activate the T2 heater through channel A it will switch to channel B after a 30 second delay. If both channels A and B fail this caution message will appear. The FADEC will not energize the T2 heater after the failure of both channels.

How many heaters are in a pitot static probe?

There are two heaters in each probe, one in the base and another in the head.

What provides control and monitoring of the probe and sensor heating?

Three separate air data sensor heater controllers (ADSHC) that provide control and monitoring.

Explain the ground mode of the air data sensor controllers (ADSHC).

On the ground with one engine generator supplying power and the probe switches are in the OFF position, the ADSHC will apply half power to the three pitot heads only. When the pilot selects the probe heater to ON, the ADSHC will then apply full power to the standby static ports and AOA sensors in addition to half power to the three pitot heads that were already powered if a engine generator was on line. The TAT and pitot bases are not heated on the ground regardless of probe switch positions.

Is there any kind of automatic heating of the AOA vanes or the static ports on the ground?

Automatic mode is when the LH and RH PROBES are in the OFF position. The AOA vanes and the static ports are not automatically heated under this condition.

When energized, what level of heating are the AOA vanes provided?

The AOA vanes are heated to full power on the ground and in flight. The probe switches activate this function.

Where are the angle of attack (AOA) vanes located?

The AOA vanes are located on each side of the aircraft below the cockpit windows.

Where is the standby pitot probe located?

The standby pitot probe is located on the left side of the nose.

Where are the alternate static ports located?

The alternate static ports are on each side of the aircraft towards the front.

Explain the flight mode of the ADSHC computers.

When the aircraft is weight-off-wheels, the ADSHCs will apply full heat to all probe heaters regardless of probe or generator switch position.

Explain the different heating modes of the pitot static probes with respect to head and base heating?

The head heater will operate at half heat on the ground and full heat in flight. The base heater operates at full heat in flight only.

Explain the heating of the standby pitot probe?

When turned on, it is provided half power for heating on the ground and full power in flight.

Are the alternate static ports heated to full heat or half heat on the ground?

With the probe switches to ON, the alternate static ports will be energized at full heat.

Where is the total air temperature (TAT) probe located?

The TAT is on the right side of the aircraft near the flight deck window.

When is the TAT probe heated and to what level?

The TAT is heated at full heat in flight only. Regardless of the probe switches, the TAT is not heated on the ground.

What would happen if a ADSHC lost power?

All probes connected to that ADSHC would revert to full power.

Are any of the ADSHCs applying power to the probes or sensors when the aircraft is at the gate with just external power or APU power and the probe switches in the OFF position. What if the probes switches are selected ON?

In the OFF position nothing is being powered. With the switches selected ON, the ADSHCs will apply half power to the three pitot heads, full power to the standby static ports and angle of attack sensors. The TAT and pitot bases are not heated on the ground.

What is heated under these conditions?

- On the ground with external power and the probe switches OFF.

- On the ground with an engine generator operating and probe switches OFF.

- On the ground with an engine generator operating and the probe switches ON.

- On the ground with the APU generator operating and the probe switches OFF.

- On the ground with the APU generator operating and the probe switches ON.

- In flight with the probe switches OFF.

What is the true purpose of the LH and RH PROBES switches?

These switches control AC power to the three pitot heads, standby static ports and AOAs with power to the aircraft and the aircraft on the ground. The switches don't really have a purpose airborne due to the ADSHCs providing full power to all probes and sensors.

What does a L or R PITOT HEAT amber caution message indicate?

In flight is means that the respective pitot tube or base heater is off or has failed. On the ground it means the respective pitot tube is off or failed. The difference is due to the base not being heated on the ground.

How do the flight deck windshields maintain a constant temperature?

There are four temperature controllers, one for each window, that monitor the electrical resistance of the temperature sensors in the glass. The power to the windshields is cycled on and off to maintain a certain glass temperature. A coating applied to inner surface of the outer glass panel is supplied electrical power for windshield heating.

Are the side cockpit windows anti-iced?

The side windows are de-fogged/de-misted only. They operate on one temperature schedule.

Are the forward flight deck windshields anti-iced?

Yes, anti-iced and also de-fogged/de-misted.

What windows does the LH WSHLD switch control?

It controls the left window and left windshield.

When the LH or RH WSHLD switch is placed in LOW, what happens?

The warm-up cycle begins to prevent thermal shock to the windshields and windows. After the warm-up cycle, the temperature controllers maintain a low heat level.

What would happen if a windshield or window started to overheat?

The overheat protection will remove power to the affected surface.

After a window or windshield overheat condition, how can the temperature controller be reset?

Moving the WSHLD switch to the OFF/RESET position will de-energize the windshield and window on that side and reset the temperature controller. Then select ON again.

When would you use the WSHLD HI position?

Use WSHLD HI only when LOW does not do the job.

Will the windshield test work when the WSHLD switches are in the OFF position?

No

How is the windshield and window system test completed?

The WSHLD switches should be in LOW or HI and then press and hold the TEST switch. The test passes when an amber L and R WSHLD HEAT and L and R WINDOW HEAT caution messages appear on the EICAS. A no-heat condition is simulated during the test.

If the copilot has the windshield wiper selected to LOW and the captain selects HI, who has control?

The captain will have control and the wipers will move at HI speed. If the captain selects OFF, the wipers will move at LOW speed and the copilot will then have control.

What is the wiper speed limit?

250 KIAS

What is the delay time with the wipers selected to intermittent?

Intermittent provides a 5 second delay.

Can the wipers be used on a dry windshield?

No

What does a green ICE on the EICAS indicate during flight?

Ice is detected and the anti-ice system is operational with sufficient heat.

When viewing the ANTI-ICE synoptic page what does a red wing and fuselage anti-ice duct indicate?

This indicates a overheat condition or a bleed-air leak.

What engine stages provide anti-ice bleed air?

6th and 10th

What happens when the WING ANTI-ICE switch is selected to ON?

The AILC modulates the wing anti-icing valves to maintain a constant wing leading edge temperature.

What position does the cowl anti-ice valves fail?

The valves are spring-loaded open.

How many heaters are in a pitot static probe?

There are two heaters in each probe, one in the base and another in the head.

chapter 13

Indicating and Recording (EICAS)

In what order are the messages displayed on the crew alerting system (CAS)?

The messages are prioritized by importance and occurrence.

How does the pilot know what message is the most recent on the CAS?

The most recent message is at the top of the associated list (ex. abnormal or warning).

What are the four levels of CAS messages?

- Warning
- Caution
- Advisory
- Status

How are the CRTs powered, DC or AC powered?

DC

Are the CRTs cooling fans DC or AC powered?

AC

How many CRT cooling fans does the aircraft have?

3

Do all the CRT cooling fans operate at the same time?

No, the fan that operates is determined by the proximity sensing system (PSS). The DSPLY FAN knob on the DISPLAY FAN and ARINC FAN control panel can be used to select different fans.

With just the battery master on, what limitation do you need to be aware of?

Because the CRT display fans are AC powered, the fans are not operating with just the battery master on. The limitation is 5 minutes due to no cooling airflow for the CRTs.

What is the main component responsible for getting the information to the EICAS?

The two data concentrator units (DCU). The DCUs receive information from many aircraft systems, process the information and relays it to the proper component or display.

Explain the lamp driver unit (LDU).

This unit controls the panel and glare shield switchlight illumination. The LDU has two channels for redundancy, should one channel fail the other will continue to operate. When the DCU sends a message to the EICAS the message is also sent to the LDU, which then will illuminate the appropriate switchlight.

How is the LDU tested?

The LAMP TEST switch on the miscellaneous test panel does the LDU test. Place the switch in 1 or 2 and this will test the associated LDU and panel lamps. This will illuminate most lights. For LAMP TEST 1, the FCC lights to the left of each button on the FCP will illuminate and not the right side light. The right side will illuminate with LAMP TEST 2. The DCU light on the first officers side panel will illuminate with the associated LAMP TEST (ex. LAMP TEST 1 will illuminate DCU 1).

How is the lamp light intensity set to bright or dim?

The IND LTS switch on the miscellaneous test panel sets lamp intensity.

What always accompanies the master warning?

A triple chime aural warning always accompanies the master warning.

What may also accompany a master warning?

A voice message or a dedicated tone.

How can a flashing master warning switchlight and the audio alert be cancelled?

By pressing the master warning switchlight.

What always accompanies a master caution switchlight?

A single chime always accompanies a master caution.

What does the AURAL WARN TEST switch do?

This switch is located on the miscellaneous test panel and is used to test the audio outputs of the DCUs. Position 1 tests DCU 1 and position 2 tests DCU 2. Positioning the switch in 1or 2 will begin the test for that respective DCU and voice warnings are sounded sequentially. To interrupt the test, select the test position again.

How could you disable the aural warnings of a particular DCU?

On the copilot's side panel there are two (optional third) AUDIO WARNING DISABLE switchlights. These switchlights are use to disable and silence the aural warnings of a DCU. When one DCU is disabled the other will provide aural warnings. If all DCUs are disabled, all EICAS aural warnings are disabled.

Are the GPWS and TCAS aural warnings disabled by selecting the AUDIO WARNING disable switches on the copilot's side panel?

No

Which four buttons on the EICAS control panel (ECP) will still operate if the ECP microprocessor fails?

- PRI
- CAS
- STAT
- STEP

Is there a backup to the microprocessor for the ECP?

No, there is just one processor for the ECP.

Explain the PRI button on the ECP.

The primary page will be displayed on ED2.

Explain the STAT button on the ECP.

The status page will be displayed on ED2. Pressing the button after the status page is on ED2 will cause the status messages to be removed and replaced by a white MSGS icon. If the DCU generates a new status message, the status messages will reappear with the new message at the top.

Can the CAS messages be cleared?

Pressing the CAS button during flight or on the ground with the engines running, the caution messages will be replaced by an amber MSGS icon. Caution messages cannot be boxed on the ground with the engines not operating or a single engine operating.

How can all the synoptic pages on ED2 be viewed during an ECP failure?

The STEP button will display the pages in order from left to right as displayed on the ECP.

What is the function of the MENU button on the ECP?

- The N1 reference can be set to display on the primary page.
- The fuel used can be reset.

When will the SEL, UPD and DN button on the ECP function?

Only when the MENU page is selected.

Why are the N1 fan vibration gauges not displayed immediately after engine start?

Once both engines are stabilized at idle and engine oil pressures are in the normal range, the N1 fan vibration gauges replace the oil pressure gauges. The oil pressure gauges will return upon engine shut down.

Does the N2 section of the engine have a vibration indication?

The N2 VIB gauge will be displayed on the N2 gauge when vibration exceeds a certain value.

What indications can be displayed on the N1 gauges?

- APR
- REV
- Thrust setting

These indications are displayed only when the systems are activated.

During flight when will the landing gear and flap position display be removed?

When all of the following are met:

- The wheel brake temperatures are in the normal range.
- Landing gear is up and locked.
- Flaps are up.

The gear and flap position indication will be displayed again when either is selected.

What types of messages are presented on ED2?

Status and advisory messages are displayed on ED2.

What types of messages are presented on ED1?

Warning and caution messages are displayed on ED1.

When will the APU RPM and EGT gauge be displayed?

The APU RPM and EGT gauge is displayed when the APU PWR FUEL switchlight is selected.

When is the APU door position indication displayed?

It is displayed continuously on ED2.

When will the crew oxygen display on ED2 turn amber to indicate a low quantity?

1410 PSI

During flight when will the brake temperature indicators be removed from display on ED2?

When all three of the following conditions are met:

- Landing gear is up and locked.
- All brake temperatures are normal.
- Flaps are up.

How is the DC ELEC synoptic page displayed?

Press the ELEC button on the ECP two times.

When would you most likely use the MENU page on the ECP?

Most aircraft are equipped so the outside air temperature can be set into the FMS and proper N1 takeoff power settings will be displayed. If the FMS fails, the power settings for takeoff and go around will need to be set. The fuel used will also need to be reset via the MENU page. All of this is done on the MENU page.

What does the magenta color indicate for the EICAS color logic?

Insufficient data to determine proper color-coding.

What does a light shade of cyan color indicate in reference to the EICAS color logic?

The component is operational.

Explain the color logic of the valves on the synoptic pages.

The valve is white if it is operable and amber if it is inoperable. The exception is the wing anti-ice and cowl valves. The A/ICE page does not indicate the actual position but shows the commanded position (CMD) of the control switches. This is why the valve is a cyan color.

Explain the color logic of the fuel and hydraulic pumps on their respective synoptic page.

- White - off
- Green - operating
- Amber - failed

What always accompanies a warning message?

- Flashing master warning lights on the glare shield panel.
- Triple chime.
- The switch associated with the system may have a red light or,
- A red indication on the EFIS or,
- A red indication on the synoptic page or,
- Some of these together.

What sometimes accompanies a warning message?

One or both of the following:

- Aural warning tone
- Voice message

When there is a warning message, what three things happen when either master warning switchlight is pressed?

- Stops the master warning lights from flashing.
- Silences the aural alerts.
- Resets the system for future messages.

Will a caution message be displayed above a warning message?

No, caution messages will always be displayed below any warning messages displayed on the CAS.

What always accompanies a caution message?

- Flashing master caution lights.

- Single chime.

- The EFIS will have an amber indication, and or

- The faulted switch will have an amber light, and or

- The associated synoptic page will have an amber indication.

What happens when there is a caution message and a master caution switchlight is pressed?

- Resets the CAS to allow it to annunciate another fault.

- Cancels the flashing master caution lights.

If there is more than one page of caution messages on the CAS, how are all messages viewed?

All messages are viewed by pressing the CAS button to cycle between pages.

Can an advisory message be cleared like the caution messages?

No, green advisory messages can only be cleared by deselecting the switch that created it.

What do the green advisory messages advise the crew of?

- Successful system test.

- Aircraft configuration.

- SOV closure.

Where is the white status messages presented?

On the status page directly below the advisory messages if present.

What does the white status message inform the crew of?

- When a system has been automatically or manually activated it indicates the status of the system.

- Failure of a low priority system.

How can more than one page of status messages be viewed?

More than one page of status messages can be viewed by pressing the STAT button on the ECP.

Can the status messages be cleared from view?

Pressing the STAT button a second time can clear the status messages. A white boxed MSGS icon will take their place.

Explain the phases of flight where the DCU inhibits distracting EICAS messages?

Takeoff:

- Condition 1: N1 greater that 79% and less than 100 KTS.

- Condition 2: Greater than 100 KTS.

Landing:

- Condition 3: Less than 400 feet AGL and will last until 30 seconds after touch down or greater than 400 feet on go-around.

What is the purpose of the EICAS reversionary mode?

It provides an alternate method of displaying EICAS information when ED1 or ED2 fail. It basically controls what is presented on the multi-function display (MFD). PFD or EICAS can be displayed.

What happens if ED1 fails?

The primary page automatically is transferred to ED2.

What happens if ED2 fails?

There is no automatic transfer of ED2. The pilot can use the EICAS switch on the display reversionary panel (DRP) to display the STATUS page from ED2 on the MFD.

What condition will cause the ECP to be inactive?

Automatic transfer of the primary page to ED2 or failure of ED2.

What is the location of the display reversionary panels (DRP) and what do they do?

The DRP is located on the pilot and copilot side panel. They control the presentation of the PFD or EICAS on the associated multi function display (MFD).

Explain the EICAS switch position on the DRP.

The STATUS page will be displayed on the associated MFD and the ECP will now function.

Explain the PFD position on the DRP.

If the primary flight display (PFD) fails, the PFD information can be displayed on the associated MFD.

Explain the EICAS selector on the source selection panel.

There are three positions NORM, ED1 and ED2. This knob is used if either EICAS display fails, which will allow all EICAS information to be presented on the operative ED.

- NORM - normal EICAS displays.

- ED1 - if ED2 fails this will allow all EICAS information to be viewed on ED1 and the ECP is now fully functional.

- ED2 - if ED1 fails this will allow all EICAS information to be viewed on ED2 and the ECP is now fully functional.

What would happen if ED1 was the only operative ED with ED1 selected on the source selection panel and a warning message is generated?

If ED1 were displaying a synoptic, status or menu page it would revert back to the primary page automatically.

Is there a reversionary mode for the normal information displayed on the MFD?

No

What would you do if a MFD was displaying a maintenance menu when you boarded an aircraft with no maintenance being done?

The red guarded switch on circuit breaker panel was probably accidentally turned on.

When does the flight data recorder (FDR) start recording?

The FDR starts recording when the strobe lights or beacon are turned on. It is also activated by the proximity sensing system's weight off wheels switches.

Explain the FDR EVENT button on the miscellaneous test panel.

When pressed, it marks a significant event on the FDR.

How will the FMS get the time if GPS is not available and the aircraft is equipped with a GPS clock?

The captain's clock will be primary and the copilot's clock is secondary. The pilot will have to manually set the time and this will disable the GPS clock function.

What components of the aircraft does the left side clock provide time to?

- ARINC bus
- FDR
- DCUs

During pushback and starting the engines a white FDR FAIL status message appears. What would you do?

The beacon switch is probably not on.

chapter 14

Landing Gear

How are the nose doors opened and closed?

The nose doors are mechanically attached to the gear and will always be open on the ground.

When hydraulic system 3 fails how is the nose gear released?

Pulling the manual gear release handle will release the nose gear. Hydraulic system 2 pressure will operate the actuator which will release the over center lock and lower the nose gear.

What is the range of the nose wheel steering?

The rudder pedals have a range of +/- 8 degrees and the tiller is +/- 80 degrees.

If the nose gear torque links (scissors) were disconnected how much can the nose gear deflect?

360 degrees

Describe the type of main landing gear?

It is a cantilever design and uses a shock.

What is the purpose of the shimmy damper on the main landing gear?

The shimmy damper removes vibrations created by the gear.

What should be checked on the tail bumper during the walk around?

If a tail strike has occurred then a red pin will pop out. There is an oleo strut behind the bumper and if it needs servicing a red indicator will be displayed.

How is the nose landing gear held in the up position?

The nose gear is held in the up position by an over center mechanism.

How is the nose gear held in the down position?

The nose gear is held in the down position by an over-center locking mechanism.

How is the main landing gear held in the up position?

The main landing gear is held in the up position by mechanical uplocks.

What hydraulic system powers the landing gear?

Hydraulic system 3 powers the landing gear.

Which hydraulic system powers the nose wheel steering?

Hydraulic system 3 powers the nose wheel steering.

Can you raise the landing gear lever while on the ground?

No, a solenoid lock prevents raising the gear lever on the ground. At weight-off-wheels, the PSS removes the solenoid lock so the gear can be selected up.

What would you do if on takeoff the landing gear lever would not go up?

This would occur if the solenoid lock or PSS malfunctioned. Use the down lock release button next to the gear handle to manually override the solenoid lock.

Are the main landing gear wheels stopped after liftoff?

Yes, hydraulic pressure is applied to the wheel brakes.

What is the general process of operation when the landing gear lever is selected to the up or down position?

The PSS receives the signal from the landing gear lever; it looks landing gear proximity sensors and weight-on-wheel function. If all the proper conditions are met, the PSEU will signal the selector valves to retract or extend the landing gear.

How is the landing gear extended if normal operation fails?

Refer to the checklist. The manual landing gear release handle can be used to lower the gear. When pulled it releases the main landing gear up-locks. A bypass valve relieves hydraulic system 3 pressure from the normal retraction and extension hydraulic circuits and the gear will partially extend under the gears own weight. The hydraulic system 2 pressure is routed to the nose gear uplock manual release actuator and the main landing gear auxiliary actuators.

The actuators help the main gear into the locked position. The nose gear is assisted to the down and locked position by two tension springs and airflow.

During manual landing gear extension, how is the landing gear put in the down and lock position?

After the up locks are released the nose gear pushes the nose doors open. The nose gear is locked down by the airflow and by two over-center springs. The main landing gear is assisted by free-fall and by the main landing gear auxiliary actuators (MLG AUX ACT).

What powers the main landing gear auxiliary actuators during manual gear extension?

Hydraulic system 2 pressure is used by the main landing gear auxiliary actuators during manual gear extension.

What are the possible causes if the landing gear will not extend?

Hydraulic system 3 has failed or there is a problem with the landing gear control circuitry.

After manual gear extension, do you stow the handle?

The handle is pressed and lowered to the stow position. Follow the checklist.

What is the job of the proximity sensing system (PSS)?

This is the system that consists of proximity sensors, proximity sensing electronic unit (PSEU), proximity switches and micro switches. The PSS monitors the aircraft doors, ground spoilers, thrust levers, parking brake, flap position and sequences the landing gear.

What are the jobs of the PSEU with reference to the landing gear operation?

The PSEU monitors the position of the uplocks, downlocks and the landing gear position. The hydraulic selector valves used in retracting and extending the landing gear are controlled by the PSEU.

What happens to the nose wheel steering and the anti-skid after takeoff?

The PSEU disables the nose wheel steering and anti-skid systems.

What activates the nose wheel steering and anti-skid systems upon landing?

PSEU

How are the tires protected against an overheated wheel or brake?

The main wheels have four fusible plugs in each tire. If the tire is overheated, the plugs melt and the tire deflates to prevent the tire form bursting.

Which hydraulic systems power the brakes?

The outboard brakes are powered by hydraulic system 2 and the inboard brakes are powered by hydraulic system 3.

Why are the main wheels stopped before gear retraction on takeoff?

This will stop the gyroscopic precession.

What would happen if a leak occurred in a brake line?

A hydraulic sensor that is a fuse will close to stop the loss of the system fluid.

Would there be any braking ability if hydraulic system 2 and 3 failed?

If hydraulic system 2 or 3 or both fail, each system has an accumulator that provides enough pressure for six brake applications. The anti-skid has to be selected off to have these six brake applications. There is a loss of 50% in braking when one system fails and anti-skid is available on the side that is working.

When should the brakes be serviced?

When the brake wear indicator pins are flush with the top of the indicator housing. Hydraulic system 2 and 3 must be on and the brakes applied for an accurate check of the pins. If the parking brake is on the brakes are applied.

How many brake wear pins are located on each brake assembly?

Two

How do you set the parking brake?

Press the toe brakes on both pedals and pull the parking brake.

What hydraulic systems have to be on for the parking brake to be fully applied?

Hydraulic systems 2 powers outboard brakes and hydraulic system 3 powers inboard brakes.

Does the parking brake hold when the hydraulic systems 2 and 3 are turned off?

The inboard brakes will hold for an extended period of time.

The aircraft is at the gate with hydraulic system 3A on and the parking brake applied. What brakes are applied?

The inboard brakes are applied.

The aircraft is at the gate with hydraulic system 3A on and the parking brake applied. Hydraulic system 3A is turned off and the aircraft is de-powered. Is the parking brake still applied and holding the aircraft in position?

Since hydraulic system 3 was operating prior to de-powering the aircraft, the inboard brakes will hold for an extended period of time.

In general how does the anti-skid work?

The speed of the tire and its speed of deceleration are sensed by the wheel speed transducers. This information is sent to the anti-skid control unit (ASCU) and it controls the hydraulic pressure to the brake to prevent lockup.

Explain how the anti-skid compares the speed of paired wheels?

The outboard wheel of each main gear is a pair and the inboard wheel of each main gear is a pair. If the outboard wheel of the left main rotates at a slower speed then the outboard of the right main, the anti-skid control unit releases the slower turning wheel brake. When the paired wheels reach the same speed, the brake will be reapplied.

What does the anti-skid system do when the aircraft becomes airborne?

The anti-skid control unit opens the anti-skid valves to full open to prevent wheel lock-up at touchdown.

When does the anti-skid system become operational upon landing?

At 35 knots wheel speed or after weight-on-wheels of 5 seconds.

What is the minimum speed the anti-skid is operational?

The minimum speed is 10 knots. Below this speed the anti-skid does not operate.

What is the purpose of the ARMED switch on the anti-skid control panel?

This arms the anti-skid system when both main landing gear are down and locked and the parking brake is not applied.

When is the anti-skid system tested?

The system is automatically tested before flight. When there is a problem it will be displayed on the EICAS.

If a channel of the anti-skid is inoperative, what will also not be working?

The BTMS on the inoperative channel will not be displayed.

Which set of brake peddles need to be applied before setting the parking brake?

Either the pilot or copilot brake peddles can be applied.

Will the parking brake maintain brake pressure after the No. 3 hydraulic system is turned off?

Accumulator pressure from the No. 3 hydraulic system will maintain inboard brake pressure for an extended period of time.

How is brake temperature monitored?

Brake temperature is monitored by the brake temperature monitoring system (BTMS).

What monitors the anti-skid system for faults?

The anti-skid control unit (ASCU) monitors for faults.

What is the equivalent temperature change for one unit of the BTMS?

One unit equals approximately 35°C (95°F).

At what values does the BTMS numbers change color?

- 0-6 green
- 7-14 white
- 15 or greater is red

Explain the BTMS overheat reset button.

If the BTMS system reaches the red zone, the BTMS will not reset the red brake reading even after the brakes cool. The reset button must be pressed to reset the system. If the brake is still overheated, it will not reset when the button is pressed. Maintenance should be contacted before resetting the system.

What BTMS range is required before takeoff?

The BTMS must be in the green range before takeoff.

How is the nose wheel moved by the controls?

Hydraulic system 3 moves the nose wheel. Nose wheel steering commands are transmitted by a steer-by-wire system.

How is the nose wheel centered on take off?

On takeoff the nose wheel is centered by the steering ECU generating a straight ahead command.

What could happen if the steering tiller is moved prior to landing?

A STEERING INOP caution message could appear.

How is steering accomplished if the NWS is inoperative?

The nose wheel steering is in a free castor mode. At higher ground speeds the rudder provides control. At lower ground speeds, throttle control and differential braking provide directional control.

Can a nose wheel steering fault be detected in flight?

Yes, the system is continuously monitored.

What does the landing configuration warning system monitor?

The warning system monitors:

- Thrust lever position
- Airspeed
- Flaps
- Landing gear position

When can the landing gear warning horn be muted?

There are two conditions that the horn can be muted:

- Less than 190 KIAS, flaps 0 and one thrust lever at idle.
- Less than 170 KIAS, flaps 30 and one thrust lever at idle.

When would a "too low gear" aural warning be heard?

When any of the three landing gear are not down and locked, the IAS is less than 190 KIAS and the radio altimeter reads less than 500 feet AGL.

When is the landing gear warning horn automatically inhibited?

The warning horn is automatically inhibited on takeoff for two minutes after weight-off-wheels and on takeoff with wind shear present.

What is the range of the brake pressure readouts on the hydraulics page?

- Green – 1800 to 3200 PSI.
- White – 3200 psi or greater.
- Amber – Less than 1800 PSI.
- If the data is invalid amber dashes will be displayed.

Explain the overheat detection in the main landing gear bay?

The system consists of a single heat-sensing loop the runs through the MLG wheel bin and is connected to a dual channel overheat detection unit. The overheat warnings and system faults are displayed on the EICAS. The system continuously monitors the MLG wheel bins for overheat conditions.

Explain the main landing gear bay overheat test?

The OVHT TEST simulates an overheat condition in the system. This test displays a red EICAS warning MLG BAY OVHT and creates an aural "gear bay overheat". When the OVHT TEST WARN FAIL switch is tested it simulates a failure of the MLG bay overheat detection system and displays an amber MLG OVHT FAIL caution message.

What closes the main landing gear doors?

The doors are attached to the main landing gear struts so the gear pulls the doors shut.

What is the purpose of the brush seals on the main landing gear doors and wheel bins?

They provide an aerodynamic seal.

After takeoff when will the EICAS BTMS, gear and flaps indications be removed?

30 seconds after weight off wheels and the following conditions are met:

- Flaps are up.

- BTMS indications are normal.

- Landing gear is up and locked.

What releases the gear lever solenoid lock after takeoff?

PSEU

How many nose gear doors are installed?

Three

What happens if a main landing gear or a nose landing gear proximity sensor fails?

Each gear has dual proximity sensors which means the other sensor will function.

What is required for the nose wheel steering to be activated?

- Hydraulic system 3 pressure.

- Weight on wheels signal from the PSEU.

- Nose gear down and locked.

When does the nose wheel steering conduct a built-in-test (BIT)?

The ECU will initiate a BIT test after every extension.

What will happen if the tiller is moved or rudder pedals moved excessively during the nose wheel steering BIT test?

The BIT test can fail.

chapter 15

Lighting

How many over wing emergency lights are installed?

There are two lights over each wing for a total of four.

What powers the floor track lighting?

The floor track lighting does not require power because they are photo luminescent strips. Photo luminescent strips glow in the dark after being stimulated with light.

Where are the strobe lights located?

A strobe light is located in each wing tip and one on the tail.

What lights will turn on the flight data recorder?

When the strobe or beacon switch is turned on.

What switch controls the flight deck entrance light?

The dome light switch on the MISC LTS panel.

What bus is the dome light switch on?

The dome light switch is on the hot bus.

What switch controls the pilot and copilot overhead light?

The control knob located on the pilot and copilot DM LT panel.

What lights are controlled by the RECOG/TAXI LTS switch?

This switch controls the recognition/taxi light in the wing roots.

What lights are controlled by the left and right landing light switch?

This will turn on the landing light and taxi-recognition light in the wing root for that side.

What light does the NOSE landing light switch turn on?

The single landing light on the nose landing gear strut.

What lights come on if only the left landing light is selected on?

The left landing light and the left recognition/taxi light.

Does the DOME light switch on the flight attendant panel control the dome light on the flight deck?

This switch controls the dome light between the flight attendant station and the flight deck. It is separate from the dome light switch on the flight deck.

What switch controls the boarding lights?

The ENTRANCE LIGHT switch on the flight attendant panel controls the boarding lights.

What lights make up the boarding lights?

The lights above the cabin door threshold and the lights in the first, third and fourth riser of the cabin door stairs.

After activating the boarding lights switch on the flight attendant panel, the door stair lights don't illuminate. What could be the problem?

The ENTRANCE LIGHT switch needs to be selected to bright. This is the only time the door step lights will illuminate.

How is the cargo compartment lights turned on?

The lights are turned on by a switch in each compartment.

If a cargo light switch was left on by the ground crew, would it remain on for the entire flight?

The cargo lights will only operate on the ground and is controlled by weight-on-wheels.

Is there lighting in the nose wheel well?

The nose wheel well has a light and is controlled by a switch next to the light.

Is there lighting in the main landing gear wheel wells?

Each wheel well has two lights and is controlled by the switch next to the lights.

Is there lighting in the avionics compartment?

Yes

Do the aft equipment bay and the APU compartment have lighting?

Yes

How are the ceiling and sidewall fluorescent lights in the cabin controlled?

The CEILING and SIDEWALL switches on the flight attendant's panel.

Explain the AUTO position of the NO SMKG and SEAT BELTS switches on the PASS SIGNS control panel on the flight deck.

In AUTO three things control the illumination of the signs:

- Flap position
- Gear position
- Cabin altitude

When the flaps are extended out of 0 degrees, the seat belt sign will illuminate. Both signs will illuminate when the gear is extended. When the cabin altitude exceeds 10,000 feet, both signs will illuminate.

What controls the activation of the seat belt signs and no smoking signs when cabin altitude exceeds 10,000 feet?

The cabin pressure acquisition module (CPAM). The NO SMKG and SEAT BELTS switches must be in AUTO.

Where are service compartment lights located?

- Avionics bay

- Aft equipment bay

- Forward and aft cargo compartment

- Nose gear wheel well

- Main gear wheel wells

- APU compartment

How are the emergency lights powered?

The emergency lights are powered by dedicated rechargeable batteries or aircraft electrical power.

How are the emergency lights controlled?

The emergency lights are controlled by an EMER LTS switch on the overhead panel of the flight deck and an EMERG LIGHT switch on the flight attendant panel.

Which emergency light switch overrides the other emergency light switch?

The flight attendant's switch will override the flight deck switch.

Explain the different components of the emergency light system?

- Exit signs.

- Lights in the ceiling of the cabin.

- Floor track emergency lights.

- Emergency floodlights at floor level.

- Exit signs at the floor level.

- Exterior emergency lights.

With the emergency light switch in the ARM position, when will the emergency lights illuminate?

The emergency lights will illuminate when all essential DC or essential AC power is lost after a one second delay.

Where is the exterior emergency exit signs located?

- One light is installed at the service/galley door.

- One light is installed at the cabin door.

- Each overwing exit has two lights.

At what point will the photo luminescent strips on the floor be fully charged?

The strips are fully charged after being exposed to cabin lighting for 15 minutes.

On the miscellaneous test panel explain the IND LTS switch?

This switch controls the illumination level of most indicator lights and annunciators.

Explain the LAMP TEST switch on the miscellaneous test panel?

The LAMP TEST switch is used to test all indicator and annunciator lamps.

Will the emergency lights illuminate if the flight deck EMER LTS switch is off and the EMER LTS switch on the flight attendant's panel is select to ON?

Yes

What cabin lights will illuminate to full bright if the passenger oxygen masks deploy?

The sidewall lights will illuminate to full bright.

chapter 16

Navigation

What are the different methods of tuning the radios, navigation and transponders?

- Radio tuning unit (RTU)
- FMS radio page
- Standby radio

How many DME signals is the VHF NAV system capable of receiving?

The two VHF NAV receivers can receive up to three channels each for a total of six channels.

When will the FMS not auto-tune the VHF NAV receiver?

- When NAV SOURCE is not the FMS.
- When the DME HOLD is selected on the RTU.
- If the FMS tune inhibit switch is activated.

Where are the two DME antennas located?

They are just forward of the wing leading edge on the bottom of the aircraft.

Where is the marker beacon antennas located?

The antennas are just forward of the aft equipment bay door on the bottom of the fuselage.

How would you access the main page of the RTU?

Press the selected line key twice.

What channel does DME hold use?

DME channel 2.

What are the indications that the VHF NAV is in DME hold?

- An amber H replaces the NM on the PFD and MFD. The station identifier is also removed.

- On the RTU main page an amber H is next to the DME frequency.

- On the RTU top page there is an amber H below the active frequency.

How will you know if the VOR or ADF is not receiving a signal from the station by looking at the bearing pointers on the PFD or MFD?

The bearing pointers will not be visible.

How many transponders are installed?

Two

What are the different modes of the transponders?

- Mode A – Reports aircraft identity only.

- Mode C – Reports aircraft altitude.

- Mode S – Communicates with other mode C and S transponders for the TCAS.

Where are the antennas for the transponders?

There are two antennas for each transponder, one on the upper forward fuselage and one lower forward fuselage for each transponder.

Explain the mode S of the transponder.

The ATC data link capability is used to communicate with other mode C and S transponder equipped aircraft to provide TCAS protection. This means that an aircraft's TCAS will tell the pilots to climb while the other aircraft's TCAS will tell it to descend. The transponder sends altitude data from the on side ADC when interrogated.

Explain the mode C of the transponder.

The transponder sends altitude data from the on-side ADC when interrogated.

What would happen if the transponder requests on-side altitude data from the on-side ADC, but it has failed?

The cross-side ADC data will be sent to the transponder by the RTU.

Explain the mode A of the transponder.

When the transponder is interrogated it replies with an identification code.

Transponder 2 uses which ADC?

ADC 2

What is the purpose of the enhanced ground proximity warning system (EGPWS)?

The EGPWS helps prevent controlled flight into terrain (CFIT) and provides warning of severe wind shear.

What are the features of the EGPWS?

- Mode 1-5 which is the basic GPWS.
- Excessive bank angle alert and altitude callouts, which is mode 6.
- Windshear detection and alerts, which is mode 7.
- Obstacle databases and terrain clearance floor on the MFD.

Explain the terrain clearance floor database (TCF) of the EGPWS.

This provides worldwide coverage of all airports with runways 3500 feet or longer. This feature has a protection zone around the airport that is based on the distance from the runway. The protection zone increases, as the aircraft gets closer to the airport runway.

Explain the terrain/obstacle awareness alerting and display database.

During all phases of fight, the EGPWS is predicting potential conflicts with terrain or obstacles in the flight path of the aircraft. The database includes all known obstacles higher than 100 feet AGL. The computer looks at flight path, ground speed and vertical speed to generate warnings of possible conflicts.

What MFD formats will allow terrain information to be presented?

- FMS map
- NAV sector

Does the terrain function of the EGPWS have to be displayed on the MFD to be active?

No, it is active at all times.

Can weather and terrain be displayed at the same time on the MFD?

No

How is the weather and terrain displayed on the MFD?

Press the WX/TERR button on the display control panel (DCP).

When is the terrain function active?

It is active all the time but it may not be displayed at all times.

Explain what occurs when conflicting obstacles or terrain are detected and the terrain feature is not displayed on the MFD?

The MFD range is automatically set to 10 miles and the terrain overlay is displayed. The pilots will hear "CAUTION TERRAIN or CAUTION OBSTACLE" over the speaker. The amber GRD PROX glare shield switchlight will flash.

What will happen to the radar display when a terrain/obstacle alert occurs?

The radar display on the MFD will be replaced by the terrain display. The RADAR in the top left corner of the MFD display is replaced with TERRAIN.

Can the EGPWS terrain be inhibited?

Yes, on the GRD PROX panel there is a terrain OFF switchlight.

Explain the excessive descent rate, mode 1 of the EGPWS.

This mode starts at 2,500 feet AGL using the radio altimeter. If the outer boundary is penetrated it will activate an aural "SINK RATE" and the yellow flashing EGPWS glare shield switchlight. This boundary is desensitized if the aircraft is capturing the glide slope from above or recapturing the localizer from above.

If the inner boundary is entered, this will activate the aural "WHOOP WHOOP, PULL UP" and the red flashing EGPWS switchlight on the glare shield. The aural warning will continue until the descent rate is corrected.

Explain EGPWS mode 2, excessive terrain closure rate.

If the aircraft is approaching terrain at an excessive rate, an alert will be generated. To generate this alert, the EGPWS uses the radio altimeter, vertical speed and the EGPWS databases. The aircraft can be in level flight or descending.

The two sub-modes for mode 2 are mode 2A and mode 2B.

- Mode 2A will first generate a "TERRAIN TERRAIN" aural message with the yellow GRND PROX switchlight illumination. Once the pull up envelope is entered, the aural "WHOOP WHOOP PULL UP" will sound until the envelope is exited. When the warning envelope is exited, the aural "TERRAIN TERRAIN" and yellow GRND PROX switchlight will continue until a 300 feet altitude gain or 45 seconds, or the 2,500 feet ability of the radio altimeter is exceeded.

- Mode 2B is used during normal approaches and landing. This mode is enabled when: 1. flaps are in landing configuration, 2.ILS approach and the aircraft is +/- 2 dots of both LOC and GS and 3. the first 60 seconds after takeoff. If the aircraft enters the envelope with either the gear or flaps not in landing configuration, the warnings are the same as in mode 2A. If the mode 2A envelope is entered with the gear and flaps in landing configuration, the aural "TERRAIN TERRAIN" and GRND PROX switchlight will warn the pilots until the envelope is exited.

Explain EGPWS mode 3, altitude loss after takeoff.

This mode will generate a "DON'T SINK" aural and the yellow GRND PROX glare shield light will flash and will remain on until a positive rate of climb is established. These alerts will occur during takeoff or go around when the altitude loss permitted by the computer is exceeded. This altitude loss is based on the height of the aircraft above the ground.

This mode is active during takeoff or a missed approach when the landing gear is up and the flaps are not in the landing position. When the aircraft has gained sufficient altitude or is not in the takeoff or missed approach mode, mode 3 is no longer enabled.

Explain the EGPWS mode 4, unsafe terrain clearance.

This mode uses information from the radio altimeter and compares the aircrafts position with the EGPWS database. The alerts are provided during climb out, cruise, descent and approach for insufficient terrain clearance. There are 3 sub modes for mode 4:

- **Mode 4A:** This mode keeps you from landing gear up by having a TOO LOW GEAR envelope. It also provides protection from terrain where the terrain does not rise significantly or the aircrafts descent rate is not excessive. The standard boundary begins at 500 feet AGL and up to 190 KIAS with the gear retracted; this will generate a "TOO LOW GEAR" aural and yellow glare shield light. As the airspeed increases above 190 KIAS, the envelope increases to 1,000 feet AGL and this will generate a "TOO LOW TERRAIN" aural with the yellow glare shield lights.

- **Mode 4B:** This mode keeps you from landing with the flaps in a position other than landing configuration with the gear down. The envelope begins at 1,000 feet AGL on the radio altimeter. A "TOO LOW TERRAIN" aural will first be generated with the yellow glare shield lights. If the speed is less than 159 knots at 245 feet AGL, a "TOO LOW FLAP" aural with the yellow glare shield lights is generated. The

FLAP OVRD switch can be used to silence this warning if landing at other than flaps 45 degrees is needed.

- **Mode 4C:** This mode is active on take off or go-around with the gear and flaps not in landing configuration. The envelope increases with altitude gain. This mode is used when the terrain is rising faster than the aircraft is climbing. The alert will be "TOO LOW TERRAIN" aural with the yellow glare shield lights.

Explain the EGPWS mode 5, below glide slope deviation alert.

There are basically two types of alerts when the aircraft deviates below the glide slope. The first occurs at 1.3 dots below the glide slope and is called a soft alert because the aural "GLIDESLOPE" is less than the second alert. The yellow glare shield lights will flash with the alert.

The second alert occurs at 300 feet AGL at more than 2 dots below the glide slope. This is the hard alert and is louder than the first alert. If either deviation increase, the repetition aural rate and glare shield lights will increase the rate of warning.

Can the EGPWS glide slope deviation alert be cancelled?

If either glideslope switchlight is pressed when the aircraft is below 1000 feet AGL, mode 5, below glideslope mode will be inhibited.

What radio altitudes are windshear conditions monitored by the EGPWS?

10 to 1500 feet AGL

Explain an EGPWS wind shear alert.

A windshear alert occurs when there are increasing performance conditions. This is a headwind or updraft. When these conditions exist, an amber pitch limit indicator (alpha margin indicator, AMI) and a amber WINDSHEAR will appear on the PFD. The FDs will only provide escape guidance when the TOGA button is pressed, and then it only provides GA pitch of 10 degrees. There will be a wind shear mode displayed in the FMA.

Explain an EGPWS windshear warning.

This alert occurs when there is a tailwind or downdraft, which causes decreasing performance. There will be an aural "WINDSHEAR WINDSHEAR WINDSHEAR". A red WINDSHEAR and the AMI displayed on the PFD. The FDs will provide escape guidance immediately up to 15 degrees. The FMA will indicate windshear mode.

Two seconds after the wind shear warning the autopilot will automatically disconnect. If the autopilot is engaged during these two seconds it will follow the FDs. This alert has priority over all other warnings.

Should the FD or the AMI be followed during a windshear warning?

Follow the FD and if it appears that ground contact will occur, pitch for the AMI.

What is the TCAS monitoring range?

40 NM

What are the four TCAS display threat levels and display icons?

- Other traffic: This is any traffic within the 40 NM range and is indicated by an open cyan diamond.

- Proximate traffic: Any traffic within 6 NM +/- 1200 and is indicated by a solid diamond.

- Traffic advisory (TA): Conflicting aircraft is 40 seconds from crossing paths and is indicated by a yellow solid circle.

- Resolution advisory (RA): Conflicting aircraft is 25 seconds from crossing paths and is indicated by a red box.

When will the up or down arrow appear on a TCAS aircraft symbol?

The arrow will appear when the TCAS aircraft is climbing or descending at 500 fpm or greater.

Which advisories have aural alerts?

Traffic advisory (TA) and resolution advisory (RA) have aural alerts.

What advisories are given to the pilots for traffic advisories?

- Above the VSI an amber TRAFFIC is displayed.
- The traffic is displayed on the MFDs as a solid amber circle.
- An aural "TRAFFIC TRAFFIC".

What are the two types of resolution advisories (RA)?

- Preventive RA - The RA will tell the pilot not to fly in a certain vertical direction.
- Corrective RA - The RA will tell the pilot to change the current vertical flight path.

The RA instructions will also be displayed on the PFD VSI.

How soon must the pilot initiate an RA escape maneuver?

The pilot must react within 2.5 seconds.

What happens if the TCAS determines the corrective action is not enough?

If the corrective action is not enough, the tone of the aural alert increases in urgency. The TCAS will tell the pilot to increase the climb or descent.

What is the minimum climb rate for an aural TCAS RA "CLIMB, CLIMB, CLIMB"?

The minimum is 1500 fpm (same for "DESCEND, DESCEND, DESCEND").

What should the pilot do if an "INCREASE CLIMB" is heard?

Increase climb rate to a minimum of 2500 fpm. It is the same response for "INCREASE DESCENT".

During a TCAS RA what will indicate the correct VSI to maintain?

The green arc on the VSI indicates the correct VSI to maintain.

While on an ILS, just pass the FAF you receive an RA and an aural "CLIMB, CLIMB, CLIMB", what would you do?

Execute a go around immediately responding to the RA. Make sure to configure the aircraft.

While on an ILS just pass the FAF at 1300 feet AGL, is it possible to receive a descending RA?

Yes, but at 1000 feet AGL and below the descend RA is inhibited.

When are all RAs inhibited?

- When descending and below 900 feet AGL.
- When climbing and below 1100 feet AGL.

While climbing just after takeoff and passing 1300 feet AGL, is it possible to receive a descending RA?

Yes, descending RAs are inhibited below 1200 feet AGL while climbing. Below 1200 feet AGL you need to think for yourself.

What are the three modes of the TCAS on the main page?

- STBY: All TCAS interrogations are inhibited.
- AUTO: TAs and RAs will be provided.
- TA ONLY: Only traffic advisories will be provided.

Explain the difference between REL and ABS on the TCAS main page.

- ABS displays the barometric altitude of the target aircraft.
- REL displays the altitude difference between the target aircraft and your aircraft.

Explain the TCAS test.

The test key selection is on the TCAS main page on the RTU. When selected the following will occur:

- Above the VSI will be TCAS TEST.
- The VSI scale will display an RA.
- If TCAS is selected on the MFD, the four different TCAS symbols will appear.
- There will be an aural "TCAS SYSTEM TEST OK" or "TCAS SYSTEM TEST FAIL" at the end of the test.

Explain the OTHER TRAFFIC key on the TCAS main page.

If OFF, the non-threat traffic up to 40 NM will not be displayed. Non-threat traffic is the open diamonds.

Explain the ABOVE, NORM and BELOW selections on the TCAS main page.

- NORM: The range of surveillance is 2700 feet above and below the aircraft.

- ABOVE: The range is 9900 feet above and 2700 feet below.

- BELOW: The range is 9900 feet below and 2700 feet above.

- If ABOVE and BELOW are selected the altitude range will be 9900 feet above and below.

How is the TCAS displayed on the MFD?

The TFC button on the DCP allows the TCAS to be displayed on the MFD. There will be little tick marks around the inner ring of the range marks of the MFD when the TCAS is active on the MFD.

Does the OFF mode of the radar park the antenna?

Yes

Does the radar transmit during the test mode?

No

Explain the MAP mode of the radar?

Map mode is used to map the terrain. The path attenuation alerts (PAC) and the ground clutter suppression (GCS) are disabled.

Explain the GAIN control knob.

Gain is used to adjust the color of the radar picture. NORM is the position that gives the best presentation under most conditions. Each position away from NORM adjusts the color level by one. It basically adjusts the sensitivity of the radar.

When the gain control is moved from NORM it should always be returned to NORM when finished. This is so you don't forget and you or someone else later interprets a cell incorrectly.

Explain what happens when the center of the GAIN knob (PUSH GCS) is pressed.

When the WX mode is active, the ground clutter suppression (GCS) decreases the intensity of the ground returns displayed on the radar. This allows the precipitation returns to be more accurately interpreted. The GCS will operate for 12 seconds after being activated. GCS will be displayed on the MFD radar mode line.

What is the degree range of the radar tilt?

+/-15 degrees

What is the beam width of the radar?

12 degrees

What tilt setting puts the bottom of the beam level with the horizon?

+6 degrees

Explain the auto-tilt button.

When selected, the auto-tilt feature automatically adjusts the beam for different altitudes and ranges to maintain the antenna tilt angle to the angle desired by the pilot. This is based on the previous selected tilt settings.

It reduces pilot workload by automatically readjusting the antenna tilt after a range or altitude change. When selected there will be an A next to the antenna tilt.

Explain how you would best use the auto-tilt feature of the radar.

One of the ways I found the tilt most useful is during a descent. When descending with weather in the area it is a good idea not to descend into a cell that may not be very high yet. For example, navigating around some cells of weather in IMC or night and ATC gives a descent. It is important to not descend into a cell. If the cell is lower, it could go under the radar tilt easily, especially if the tilt is not low enough.

In descents, I like to have the tilt down painting a lot of ground on the top of the range scale. This way if a lower cell is in my path the radar beam will still catch it as it will show up between the aircraft the ground display on the radar. This is where auto-tilt comes in handy. For example in the descent if the range on the radar is set to the 100NM scale and I am painting ground from 70NM to 100NM, I would press the auto-tilt and the radar would continue to paint 70NM to 100NM during the descent. If auto-tilt was not engaged, I would have to adjust the radar tilt to maintain this range. Otherwise the radar would just continue to paint more and more of the range back to the aircraft as the aircraft descended. If the aircraft is descending at 2800fpm or so, it is easy to descend into a lower area of weather if that weather goes under the radar tilt in the descent.

Explain the STAB radar button.

This turns on or off the stabilization function. When un-stabilized an amber USTB is displayed on the radar line. The stabilization automatically adjusts the radar to maintain the selected antenna tilt with the horizon as the aircraft turns and makes pitch changes.

Explain the SEC button on the radar.

The sector scan has to selections, +/-60 and +/-30 degrees and the SEC button is used to select the modes. SEC allows for a faster refresh rate.

Explain the XFR button on the radar control panel.

This button determines which pilot has control of the radar range with the standard installation. The pilot who has control will have range markers that are white and the pilot without control will have amber. If the non-controlling pilot has their range at something that does not match the controlling pilot's, they will have a message RADAR NOT AT THIS RANGE on their MFD. They will have to select the same range to have a radar display.

The captain lost control of the radar range on his MFD, what would you do?

Select the XFR button on the radar control panel and let the FO change the radar range.

What two MFD formats allow the radar to be overlaid?

- NAV SECTOR
- FMS MAP

Explain the path attenuation correction and alert (PAC).

When an area of weather absorbs a significant amount of the radar energy, the radar sensitivity is corrected to give an accurate image. If the cell of weather uses the full correction ability of the radar, a PAC alert will be given. A PAC alert is given by displaying a yellow arc at the top of the radar display. This is an area with a shadow and should be avoided.

chapter 17

Oxygen

Where is the oxygen cylinder for the flight deck located?

The bottle is in a closet behind circuit breaker panel number one

How would you know if the flight deck oxygen bottle had an overpressure situation?

There is a discharge indicator on the left forward side of the fuselage.

When will the OXY LO PRESS message be displayed?

The message will display when the flight deck oxygen bottle is less than 960psi.

What is the source of supplemental oxygen for the flight deck?

An oxygen cylinder supplies the three oxygen masks on the fight deck.

What is the fully charged pressure of the flight deck oxygen bottle?

1850 PSI

What are the three modes of the flight deck oxygen masks?

- Normal diluted demand: Ambient air is mixed with the oxygen.
- 100% pure oxygen.
- 100% continuous flow under pressure.

How would you know if you have enough oxygen pressure for a flight with a jumpseater?

Use the associated chart to check based on outside temperature. It is probably in your POH.

Where is the oxygen pressure indications located?

Indications are displayed on the EICAS, the oxygen services panel and a gauge on the bottle SOV.

How would you know if the oxygen bottle had an overpressure condition?

The EICAS PSI reading would be an amber 0 with an amber OXY LO PRESS EICAS message. The green oxygen discharge indicator on the forward left side of the aircraft would probably indicate a discharge.

At what cylinder pressure would the high pressure relief valve discharge the pressure overboard?

When the bottle pressure reaches 2,500 to 2,775 PSI the valve will discharge the bottle pressure.

Explain how to test the crew oxygen mask.

Press the TEST button on the oxygen mask container and hold it during the complete test. This will cause the flow blinker to display a yellow cross and then disappear, which indicates that oxygen is flowing. Then squeeze the red release levers; this will cause the harness to inflate. Press the emergency flow control knob to check if continuous flow is available. Make sure the emergency flow control knob is in 100%.

Explain the white ON flag located in the door of the crew oxygen mask container.

When the mask is out of the container and in use, a white ON flag is in view on the left door. This indicates the oxygen shutoff valve is open.

What position should the NORMAL 100% lever be in at all times when the mask is not in use?

It should be in the 100% position. When the mask is needed, the situation can be assessed and if the N (normal) position for diluted oxygen can be used, then the pilot can select it.

How is the crew oxygen supply pressure adjusted on the mask?

The emergency flow control knob adjusts the pressure. The knob is rotated to adjust the supply pressure. EMERGENCY provides constant flow of oxygen at a low positive pressure.

At high cabin altitudes can the oxygen in the crew oxygen mask be diluted with ambient air?

When the cabin altitude reaches 30,000 feet, the flow will be 100% oxygen in either NORMAL or 100%.

How can the crew oxygen mask be purged of smoke?

Press the emergency flow control knob momentarily on the mask to provide a burst of positive air pressure.

How is the crew oxygen mask microphone selected?

Select the mask microphone by the MASK/BOOM switch on the ACP.

When will the passenger oxygen masks automatically deploy?

The masks will automatically deploy when the CPAM detects a cabin altitude of 14,000 feet.

When the PASS OXY switchlight on the flight deck is illuminated, does that mean the passenger masks have deployed?

It means that the signal has been sent to drop the masks but they may not have dropped. It indicates the oxygen doors are open.

How many times can an oxygen generator be used?

The oxygen generator can be used one time.

What starts the flow of oxygen to the passenger masks?

When the passenger pulls the mask down, the lanyard is pulled and starts the chemical reaction, which provides the oxygen.

How can the passenger oxygen masks be manually deployed?

Pressing the PASS OXY switchlight on the flight deck normally deploys the masks. The flight attendant can use a pin (special pin, safety pin, etc.) to manually deploy each individual mask.

Why should the oxygen generator not be touched after activation?

The generator can reach temperatures of 500°F (260 C) when in use.

The flight attendant calls up during the use of passenger oxygen and tells you she smells a burning odor coming from the oxygen generators, is this an indication of a problem?

The generators may create a burning smell and this is normal.

What controls the automatic dropping of the passenger masks?

The cabin pressurization acquisition module (CPAM) controls the automatic deployment of the passenger oxygen masks. When the CPAM detects a cabin altitude of 14,000 feet, it sends an electrical signal to the containers to release the masks.

What is the duration of the passenger oxygen once it is activated?

Duration of the oxygen is approximately 13 minutes.

How many passenger masks are on each side of the cabin?

Three masks are on the right side (FO side) and two masks are on the left side (CA side) of the aircraft.

Besides above the passenger seats, are there any other passenger oxygen masks in the cabin?

One passenger oxygen mask located in the lavatory and one at both flight attendant stations.

How many portable oxygen bottles are located in the cabin?

Two portable oxygen bottles are located in the cabin, one aft and another forward.

What are the components of the portable oxygen system?

- Protective breathing equipment (PBE)

- Portable oxygen cylinders

- Portable mask

What are the locations of the PBEs?

There is usually one on the flight deck and a couple in the cabin. (Refer to your company manuals).

What does the crew oxygen mask blinker indicate?

A yellow cross is displayed when the harness inflates or oxygen is flowing. The blinker will be black when there is no oxygen flow.

What does the OXY ON flag indicate?

This flag indicates the mask is out of the storage container and the oxygen SOV is open.

Explain the operation of the EMERG flow control knob on the mask?

The knob is pressed during the mask test to check if continuous flow is operating. The knob can be rotated to provide 100% oxygen under positive pressure. The control knob can then be rotated to adjust the pressure supply to the mask.

chapter 18

Power Plant

What type of engines is on the CRJ700?

The CF34-8C1 or CF34-8C5B1 engine is on the CRJ700.

What is the acronym FADEC?

FADEC is the acronym for full authority digital engine control.

Explain the compressor and turbine section?

The N1 fan is connected to a four stage low pressure turbine. The axial flow compressor has 10 stages (N2) and is connected to a two stage high-pressure turbine.

What is the takeoff thrust rating?

12,670 pounds

What is the APR thrust rating?

The thrust is increased to 13,790 pounds.

How are the N1 and N2 sections connected?

The N1 and N2 sections are independent.

How much of the thrust does the bypass N1 airflow produce on takeoff?

80%

Do the thrust reversers direct the core or bypass airflow forward to assist in braking?

The bypass airflow is diverted forward.

What does the variable guide (VG) control?

This system changes the position of the first four stages of the stator vanes and the inlet guide vanes. This is what regulates airflow across the compressor section.

How does the VG system move?

Fuel is metered by the FADEC to hydraulically change the angles. The VG system inlet guide vanes are actually moved by mechanical linkage by actuators that are moved hydraulically by high pressure fuel.

What is the purpose of the VG system?

The VG system improves the efficiency of the compressor and helps to avoid surge and stalls of the engine.

Explain the operability valve (surge valve).

The surge valve is controlled by FADEC fuel metering to hydraulically operate the valve. This valve will unload bleed air from the compressor during high compressor loading like engine starts.

What are some of the items driven by the engine mounted accessory gearbox?

- FADEC alternator.
- Engine oil pump.
- Air turbine starter (ATS).
- Engine fuel pump and fuel metering unit.
- Engine driven hydraulic pump.
- IDG.

The standby FADEC channel doesn't provide control except under one condition. What is that condition?

The standby channel processes all input information but will only provide control during an engine over speed. When an over speed occurs the standby and active FADEC channel will command the shutoff valve in the fuel metering unit to close.

When will a FADEC channel switch from standby to controlling?

If the controlling channel fails, the standby will become controlling automatically. During every second engine start the channels switch roles.

What is the power source of the FADEC system?

If the N2 is greater than 50% the FADEC alternator on the accessory gearbox supplies power to both channels of the FADEC. When the N2 is less than 50% the FADEC is powered by the aircraft's electrical system.

What is required for the starter to operate?

- DC electrical power
- Pressurized air

What type of engine starter does the CRJ have?

The engine starter is an air turbine starter.

What are the sources that can provide air to start the engines?

- External air cart
- APU
- Cross bleed start

What is the purpose of the start valve?

The valve meters the amount of air to the starter, which controls the rate of engine acceleration.

What are the five N2 idle settings?

- Flight idle
- Approach idle
- Landing idle
- Reverse idle
- Ground idle

What are the two ways the start valve will close?

- Press the STOP switchlight on the start ignition panel.
- When the N2 RPM is above 50%.

Explain flight idle.

Thrust lever is at idle, flaps are 20 degrees or less and landing gear is up.

Explain approach idle.

This is when the gear is down and flaps greater than 20 degrees. Approach idle will allow the engine to achieve go around thrust in the least amount of time.

Explain landing idle.

This idle occurs at touchdown and will keep the N2 speed up a little until reverser deployment. This allows the engine to achieve reverse idle quickly. If the reversers are not deployed upon landing the FADEC will maintain landing idle for 5 seconds and then it will switch to ground idle.

Explain reverse idle.

When weight-on-wheels or wheel rotation is sensed, reverse idle will increase the N2 core speed once the thrust reversers are actuated.

Explain ground idle.

This is the lowest idle and occurs while on the ground. It will change with temperature and altitude.

How much of a loss of power on one engine will cause the FADEC to increase N1 on the other engine?

If there is a difference of 15% N1, the FADEC will increase N1 on the other engine. The amount of the increase depends on the thrust lever position at failure. During TOGA it will be APR power. With CLIMB detent set, it will be MCT and with CRUISE set it will be a proportional thrust increase.

At what point is the APR armed?

APR is armed when both engines are within 8% of takeoff power during takeoff. When the approach bit is set the APR is armed for the go-around.

What happens to the APR when the power is set to MAX POWER?

The APR is activated and the APR icon will be displayed in the N1 gauge.

What two conditions will display the APR icon in the center of the N1 gauge of an operating engine?

- An engine failure.
- The thrust lever is set to MAX POWER.

How is flex thrust displayed on the N1 gauge?

- FLX in the N1 gauge
- Magenta caret
- Digital display

Which engine is the master for the engine sync?

The left engine is the master.

When the power is set in the CLIMB detent, what happens to the power setting if an engine fails?

The N1 on the operating engine will increase to MCT.

What does the HIGH POWER switchlight do?

This will set both engines to a single engine fuel flow depending on the thrust lever position. If the thrust levers are in CLIMB, pressing HIGH POWER will set MCT. If the thrust levers are in TOGA, pressing HIGH POWER will set APR.

Explain engine synchronization.

When the thrust levers are in the cruise range the FADEC can sync the N1 or N2. Selection of N1 or N2 is done on the ENGINES control panel. The left engine is the master and the right is the slave. The N1 selected position allows the FADEC to match N1s if the right engine N1 is within 1.5% of the left. If the switch is in the N2 position, the FADEC will match core speed if the right engine N2 is within 7.5% of the left engine.

When will the GA mode be armed and presented on the thrust mode annunciation?

On approach with the gear down or the flaps greater than 20 degrees.

At what point is the takeoff thrust N1 locked?

The normal rated N1 is continuously updated but at 65 knots the takeoff N1 is locked in.

At what point is the takeoff thrust N1 unlocked?

At 400 feet AGL or when the thrust levers are moved from TOGA.

Is flex thrust continuously updated on the ground?

No

Where are the indications of the chip detector and impending oil filter bypass?

In the aft equipment bay.

When will the EICAS status message L(R) OIL LEVEL LO be displayed?

If the engines are operating and the oil quantity is less than 57% or the engines are not operating and the quantity is less than 80%.

How is the engine oil tanks replenished with oil?

In the aft equipment bay is an oil tank that can provide pressurized refilling of oil to the engine oil tanks.

What redundancy is built into the oil pressure indications?

A pressure transmitter and a pressure switch monitor engine oil pressure. If the pressure switch detects low oil pressure, it will display an EICAS L (R) ENG OIL PRESS warning message. When the pressure transmitter detects low oil pressure, the oil pressure digital readout changes to red.

What is required to open the start valve?

DC electrical power and pneumatic pressure is required to open the start valve.

At what N2% will the start valve close and the starter disengage?

50% N2

How does the FADEC select which ignition system is used for an engine start?

The FADEC will alternate the ignition systems to continuously verify operation.

During engine starts when do the igniters begin firing?

The igniters begin firing when the thrust lever is moved from shutoff to idle.

Up to what RPM can the starter be engaged?

45% N2

What RPM will the starter dry motor the engine?

The starter can dry motor the engine up to 30% N2.

Explain the automatic hot start protection while on the ground.

When the ITT exceeds 815 before reaching idle (ground only), the FADEC will stop the ignition and close the fuel-metering valve to terminate the start. The starter will not de-energize.

Explain the automatic relight function of the engine?

If the FADEC detects an engine spool down the FADEC will begin an automatic relight. The relight will continue until the engine is not turning enough to relight.

What does an advisory message L or R AUTO IGNITION indicate?

The ignition is automatically activated by the FADEC.

Are the ignition systems DC or AC powered?

Ignition A and B are AC ignition systems. Ignition system B has a static inverter that turns DC to AC power.

What are the power sources for ignition A and B?

- The AC essential bus powers ignition A.
- The battery bus powers ignition B through a static inverter.

Does continuous ignition activate ignition A or B?

Both ignitions are energized.

What controls the ignition system?

The FADEC automatically controls the ignition system.

Explain the automatic hung start protection.

When the N2 is very slow before reaching idle but after light off the start will be terminated by the FADEC. The start will terminate by ceasing ignition and closing the fuel-metering valve. The starter will not de-energize.

What is the ITT limit during engine starts?

The ITT limit varies depending on the start conditions.

When is the CONT IGNITION automatically engaged?

CONT IGNITION is automatically engaged by the FADEC and the stall warning computer during high AOA. When the airflow to the engine is disturbed, the FADEC will activate both ignitions and open the operability valve to unload the compressor.

What does an illuminated CONT IGNITION switchlight indicate?

Both igniters on both engines are activated.

When must continuous ignition be used?

- Takeoff and landings on contaminated runways.
- Flight in moderate or heavier rain.

- Flight in the vicinity of thunderstorms.

- Flight in moderate or heavier turbulence.

What happens if a flameout is detected by the FADEC?

The FADEC will try to relight the engine. The L AUTO IGNITION and R AUTO IGNITION advisory message will be presented on the EICAS and both ignition systems will be energized.

What happens if the N2 drops below the relight envelope?

The FADEC turns off the ignition and fuel to that engine and stops the auto relight. A caution message L (R) ENG FLAMEOUT is presented. When the engine thrust lever is placed to SHUTOFF the EICAS L or R ENG SHUTDOWN message is presented.

Explain the engine overspeed protection.

If the N2 attains 107% the FADEC will sense an overspeed condition. The FADEC will shut off fuel to the engine to initiate an engine flameout. The ignition will be activated because of the flameout. When the N2 is below the overspeed setting the FADEC will provide normal fuel flow again to relight the engine.

How is the reverser-translating cowl moved?

Hydraulic actuators move the translating cowls. The left reverser is powered by hydraulic system 1 and the right by hydraulic system 2.

What is required for thrust reverser deployment?

- Weight on wheels.

- Thrust levers at idle.

- Reversers armed.

When will the N1 VIB gauge change to amber?

1.75

Are there any EICAS indications for VIB problems?

No

Is there a mechanical connection between the thrust levers and the fuel metering unit (FMU)?

No

How is thrust lever position sent to the FADEC?

The rotary variable differential transformers (RVDT) send thrust lever position electronically to the FADEC.

The TOGA position is used to set what power?

Takeoff power, flex power and go around power.

When will the FADEC activate ignition?

- Engine start.
- Airflow disruption.
- Based on AOA information from the stall protection system computer during high AOA.

What would happen if both FADEC channels on an engine failed?

The respective engine would flame out.

What drives the FADEC dedicated alternator?

Engine accessory gearbox.

If the left FADEC completely fails can the right FADEC assume control?

No

When FLEX thrust is set and an engine fails, what will the operating engine accelerate to?

The power goes from FLEX to APR, which can be a big increase in power.

What happens if fuel is introduced when ITT is above 120 degrees during ground starts?

The start will be aborted by the FADEC.

What happens if fuel is introduced when ITT is above 90 degrees during air starts?

The FADEC will continue the start.

If a thrust reverser deploys in flight what will the FADEC do to the engine?

The FADEC will slow the engine to idle. Emergency-stow switchlights and a thrust lever retarding mechanism are not installed.

When the thrust levers are moved to cutoff, what actually shuts off the fuel?

The SOV on the fuel metering unit closes to shutoff fuel when the thrust levers are moved to shutoff.

When the engine fire switchlight is pressed, what actually shuts off the fuel?

The engine fuel feed SOV closes when the engine fire switchlight is pressed.

What are the different ways to stop fuel flow to the engine?

- Shut off the thrust lever.

- Press the fire switchlight on the glare shield panel.

What is the purpose of the fuel oil heat exchanger?

The exchanger warms the fuel and cools the engine oil.

What valves open when the engine START switchlight is pressed?

- ISOL valve.

- Start valve for the engine that is being started.

Which engine components are monitored for vibration?

The N2 core section and the N1 fan section.

When will the N1 fan vibration gauges be displayed on the EICAS?

The gauges will be displayed when oil pressures are normal and both engines are operating.

Can the thrust levers be moved forward after the thrust reverser levers have been activated?

No, the thrust levers are locked at idle.

What does the FADEC do if there is an inadvertent thrust reverser deployment?

The FADEC electronically selects idle thrust. The thrust lever must be moved to idle but the thrust is already at idle.

How is the N2 vibration levels displayed?

The N2 vibration level is not presented like the N1 VIB gauges. The N2 vibration is always monitored but is only displayed when N2 is outside a target limit.

When there is excessive N2 vibration, how will it be displayed?

There is no EICAS caution message, but there will be an amber VIB in the N2 gauge. The N2 gauge will also turn amber.

What is the color ranges of the oil temperature indications?

- Green: -40-155°C
- Amber: 156 to 163°C
- Red: 164°C and above

At what oil pressure indication will the N1 vibration gauges be removed?

25 PSI

What is the color ranges of the oil pressure indications?

- Red: 0-24 psi
- Green: 25-116 psi
- Amber: 117 psi or higher

chapter 19

Water and Waste

Do the forward and aft water systems share a common line between them?

No

How many potable water tanks are on the CRJ 700?

One forward and one aft for a total of two potable water tanks.

How is the forward water storage tank heated to prevent freezing?

The tank is located in the forward galley of the cabin so heating is not necessary.

Where is the aft water tank located?

The aft water tank is in the tail section under the floor.

How does the aft water tank prevent the water from freezing?

It is heated to prevent freezing.

Where are the external service panels for the potable water located?

The service panel for the forward potable water is located on the lower right forward side of the aircraft just aft of the service door. The service panel for the aft potable water system is on the aft left side of the aircraft.

What pressurizes the water systems?

Under normal conditions air from the ECS is used. If bleed air from the ECS is not available pressurized air is provided by a back up compressor. Also on the aft service panel there is a connection that allows an external source to pressurize the water system.

Where is the galley control panel located?

The galley control panel is in the forward galley.

What is powered by the FWD (AFT) ON/OFF switchlight on the galley control panel?

- Water level sensor system
- Heater systems
- Compressor

What do the drain fault lights on the galley control panel indicate?

The system has detected a fault in the drain mast associated with that system.

What does the DIAGNOSTIC light on the galley control panel indicate?

A fault in the system has been detected and is not critical but the functions of the system my be reduced.

Sources

- Bombardier Inc. - Canadair Regional Jet Pilot Reference Manual

- Flight Safety CL-65 CRJ 700 Series Flight Crew Operating manual Vol. 2

Author Biography

Aaron Boone's certificates include ATP, CFI, CFII and MEI. He is type rated in the CL-65, E-120, CE-500 and the CE-560XL. Prior to his current position as a corporate pilot he was an airline captain for a large regional airline, a flight instructor and a freight pilot.

With a BA in Psychology he understands what it takes to get ready for a checkride and to keep your CRJ systems knowledge in top shape. Aaron used his study system through college to greatly improve the efficiency of his study time and improve his grades.

Made in the USA
Middletown, DE
07 November 2019